3 -99

Getting Started with Hazelcast

An easy-to-follow and hands-on introduction to the highly scalable data distribution system, Hazelcast, and its advanced features.

Mat Johns

[PACKT] open source ✳
PUBLISHING   community experience distilled

BIRMINGHAM - MUMBAI

Getting Started with Hazelcast

First published: July 2013

Production Reference: 1190813

Published by Packt Publishing Ltd.
Livery Place
35 Livery Street
Birmingham B3 2PB, UK

ISBN 978-1-78216-730-3

www.packtpub.com

Cover Image by Artie Ng (artherng@yahoo.com.au)

Credits

Author

Mat Johns

Reviewers

Nishant Chandra

Fuad Malikov

Acquisition Editor

Mary Nadar

Commissioning Editor

Subho Gupta

Technical Editors

Dylan Fernandes

Mrunmayee Patil

Project Coordinator

Akash Poojary

Proofreader

Maria Gould

Indexer

Hemangini Bari

Graphics

Abhinash Sahu

Production Coordinator

Aparna Bhagat

Kirtee Shingan

Cover Work

Kirtee Shingan

About the Author

Mat Johns is an agile software engineer, hands-on architect, and a general technologist based in London. His experience with the Web reaches all the way back to his misspent youth and some rather hacktastic code, but eventually he grew up to graduate from the University of Southampton with a Masters in Computer Science with Distributed Systems and Networks. He has worked for a number of startups on various web projects and systems since then and nowadays he specializes in designing and creating high performance and scalable web services, currently in the Internet TV world.

Away from technology, he is an avid explorer and endeavors to seek out new destinations and adventures as much as possible. He is also a qualified yacht skipper and regularly races in, around, and beyond the Solent.

You can follow him on Twitter at @matjohns.

I would like to dedicate this book to my incredible parents and grandparents (Trevor, Alison, David, and Sheila) as without your encouragement and support over so many years, this book would not have been possible.

About the Reviewers

Nishant Chandra is a principal software engineer at Boomerang Commerce. His main interests are in building scalable software, SOA, data mining, and mobile. He has been working on e-commerce applications based on large J2EE and peer-to-peer technologies. He is an active blogger (http://n-chandra.blogspot.in/) and contributes to open source projects. Other than software technology, he is also interested in analytics, product management, Internet marketing, and startups.

In the past, Nishant has worked at Amazon.com and Adobe Inc.

> I would like to thank my wife, Vibhuti, for her encouragement and patience during the review process.

Fuad Malikov is CTO and co-founder of Hazelcast. Prior to Hazelcast, he worked on J2EE projects as a technology consultant in financial and telecom industries. He was an IT architect at IBM, developing a J2EE-based core-banking system for one of the biggest banking transformation projects in Europe. He loves math and has a bronze medal from the International Mathematical Olympiad. He holds a B.Sc.in Computer Engineering from Bogazici University, Istanbul.

www.PacktPub.com

Support files, eBooks, discount offers, and more

You might want to visit www.PacktPub.com for support files and downloads related to your book.

Did you know that Packt offers eBook versions of every book published, with PDF and ePub files available? You can upgrade to the eBook version at www.PacktPub.com and as a print book customer, you are entitled to a discount on the eBook copy. Get in touch with us at service@packtpub.com for more details.

At www.PacktPub.com, you can also read a collection of free technical articles, sign up for a range of free newsletters, and receive exclusive discounts and offers on Packt books and eBooks.

http://PacktLib.PacktPub.com

Do you need instant solutions to your IT questions? PacktLib is Packt's online digital book library. Here, you can access, read, and search across Packt's entire library of books.

Why Subscribe?

- Fully searchable across every book published by Packt
- Copy and paste, print and bookmark content
- On demand and accessible via web browser

Free Access for Packt account holders

If you have an account with Packt at www.PacktPub.com, you can use this to access PacktLib today and view nine entirely free books. Simply use your login credentials for immediate access.

Table of Contents

Preface

Hazelcast is an innovative new approach to data, in terms of storage, processing, and distribution; it provides an accessible solution to the age-old problem of application and data scalability. *Getting Started with Hazelcast* introduces this great open source technology in a step-by-step, easy-to-follow manner, from the why to the how to wow!

What this book covers

Chapter 1, What is Hazelcast?, helps us to get introduced with the technology, its place in an application's stack, and how it has evolved from traditional approaches to data.

Chapter 2, Getting Off the Ground, helps us start coding and get acquainted with the standard distributed data store collections on offer.

Chapter 3, Going Concurrent, helps us expand to look at more distributed and concurrent capabilities we can bring into our applications.

Chapter 4, Divide and Conquer, helps us look at how data is split up and split across many nodes to provide both performance and resilience.

Chapter 5, Listen Out, helps us discover that we can register to receive notifications from the cluster to enable our application to be aware of the goings on.

Chapter 6, Spreading the Load, helps us move beyond the data storage, and we investigate the distributed execution service and how Hazelcast is more than just a database.

Chapter 7, Typical Deployments, helps us explore the various ways we can use or install Hazelcast into our application or infrastructure, looking at the architectural decisions, reasons, and trade-offs behind each one.

Chapter 8, From the Outside Looking In, helps us look at popular alternative access we have to our data rather than using the provided drivers for integrating with a Hazelcast cluster.

Chapter 9, Going Global, helps us explode onto the world stage using the public cloud infrastructure and asynchronous remote replication to take our data all around the globe.

Chapter 10, Playing Well with Others, helps us bring the technology together with popular companion frameworks to see how we might start to bring the technology to work with legacy applications.

Appendix, Configuration Summary, helps us overview of the configurations we have used throughout the book.

What you need for this book

Hazelcast is a Java-based technology so you will need a Java development environment (ideally Java 6 or newer) and use of a Java source code editor, preferably an IDE.

Who this book is for

If you are software architect or Java developer looking to make your applications more scalable or looking to move into the cloud, Hazelcast is a technology you should strongly consider. This book seeks to provide an easy introduction to this innovative data centric framework and into its new way of thinking.

Conventions

In this book, you will find a number of styles of text that distinguish between different kinds of information. Here are some examples of these styles, and an explanation of their meaning.

Code words in text are shown as follows: "A GET method to retrieve an entry, returning a 200 OK response for keys that hold a value and 204 No Content for keys that do not."

A block of code is set as follows:

```
$ pyton memcache_example.py
{'country': 'GB', 'name': 'London', 'population': 8174100}

$ php -f memcache_example.php
array (
  'name' => 'London',
  'country' => 'GB',
  'population' => 8174100,
)
```

Any command-line input or output is written as follows:

```
$ curl -v -X POST -H "Content-Type: text/plain" -d "bar" \
http://127.0.0.1:5701/hazelcast/rest/maps/test/foo

< HTTP/1.1 204 No Content
< Content-Length: 0
```

New terms and **important words** are shown in bold. Words that you see on the screen, in menus or dialog boxes for example, appear in the text like this: "Now, just go the **File** menu and click on **New**".

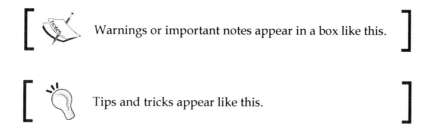

> Warnings or important notes appear in a box like this.

> Tips and tricks appear like this.

Reader feedback

Feedback from our readers is always welcome. Let us know what you think about this book — what you liked or may have disliked. Reader feedback is important for us to develop titles that you really get the most out of.

To send us general feedback, simply send an e-mail to feedback@packtpub.com, and mention the book title through the subject of your message.

If there is a topic that you have expertise in and you are interested in either writing or contributing to a book, see our author guide on www.packtpub.com/authors.

Customer support

Now that you are the proud owner of a Packt book, we have a number of things to help you to get the most from your purchase.

Downloading the example code

You can download the example code files for all Packt books you have purchased from your account at http://www.packtpub.com. If you purchased this book elsewhere, you can visit http://www.packtpub.com/support and register to have the files e-mailed directly to you.

Errata

Although we have taken every care to ensure the accuracy of our content, mistakes do happen. If you find a mistake in one of our books—maybe a mistake in the text or the code—we would be grateful if you would report this to us. By doing so, you can save other readers from frustration and help us improve subsequent versions of this book. If you find any errata, please report them by visiting http://www.packtpub.com/support, selecting your book, clicking on the **errata submission form** link, and entering the details of your errata. Once your errata are verified, your submission will be accepted and the errata will be uploaded to our website, or added to any list of existing errata, under the Errata section of that title.

Piracy

Piracy of copyright material on the Internet is an ongoing problem across all media. At Packt, we take the protection of our copyright and licenses very seriously. If you come across any illegal copies of our works, in any form, on the Internet, please provide us with the location address or website name immediately so that we can pursue a remedy.

Please contact us at copyright@packtpub.com with a link to the suspected pirated material.

We appreciate your help in protecting our authors, and our ability to bring you valuable content.

Questions

You can contact us at questions@packtpub.com if you are having a problem with any aspect of the book, and we will do our best to address it.

Trademarks

- Hazelcast is a trademark of Hazelcast Inc.
- Amazon AWS and EC2 are registered trademarks of Amazon Web Services Inc and/or its affiliates.
- Java is a registered trademark of Oracle Inc and/or its affiliates.
- Puppet is a registered trademark of Puppet Labs Inc.
- Chef is a registered trademark of OpsCode Inc.

1
What is Hazelcast?

Most, if not all, applications need to store some data, some applications far more than others. By holding this book in your eager hands and starting to flip through its pages, it might be safe to assume you have previously worked to architect, develop, or support applications more towards the latter end of that scale. We could imagine that you are all too painfully familiar with the common pitfalls and issues that tend to crop up around scaling or distributing your data layer. But to make sure we are all up to speed, in this chapter, we shall examine:

- Traditional approaches to data persistence
- How caches have helped improve performance, but bring about their own problems
- Hazelcast's fresh approach to the problem
- A brief overview its generic capabilities
- Summary of what type of problems we might solve using it

Starting out as usual

In most modern software systems, data is the key. For more traditional architectures, the role of persisting and providing access to your system's data tends to fall to a relational database. Typically this is a monolithic beast, perhaps with a degree of replication, although this tends to be more for resilience rather than performance.

For example, here is what a traditional architecture might look like (which hopefully looks rather familiar).

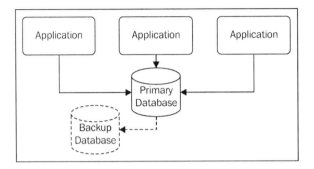

This presents us with an issue in terms of application scalability, in that it is relatively easy to scale our application layer by throwing more hardware at it to increase the processing capacity. But the monolithic constraints of our data layer would only allow us to do this so far before diminishing returns or resource saturation stunted further performance increases; so what can we do to address this?

In the past and in legacy architectures, the only solution would be to increase the performance capability of our database infrastructure, potentially by buying a bigger, faster server or by further tweaking and fettling the utilization of currently available resources. Both options are dramatic, either in terms of financial cost and/or manpower; so what else could we do?

Data deciding to hang around

In order for us to gain a bit more performance out of our existing setup, we can hold copies of our data away from the primary database and use these in preference wherever possible. There are a number of different strategies we could adopt, from transparent second-level caching layers to external key-value object storage. The detail and exact use of each varies significantly depending on the technology or its place in the architecture, but the main desire of these systems is to sit alongside the primary database infrastructure and attempt to protect it from an excessive load. This would then tend to lead to an increased performance of the primary database by reducing the overall dependency on it. However, this strategy tends to be only particularly valuable as a short-term solution, effectively buying us a little more time before the database once again starts to reach saturation. The other downside is that it only protects our database from read-based load; if our application is predominately write-heavy, this strategy has very little to offer.

So our expanded architecture could look a bit like the following figure:

Therein lies the problem

However, in insulating the database from the read load, we have introduced a problem in the form of a cache consistency issue, in that, how does our local data cache deal with changing data underneath it within the primary database? The answer is rather depressing: it can't! The exact manifestation of any issues will largely depend on the data needs of the application and how frequently the data changes; but typically, caching systems will operate in one of the two following modes to combat the problem:

- **Time bound cache**: Holds entries for a defined period (time-to-live or TTL)
- **Write through cache**: Holds entries until they are invalidated by subsequent updates

Time bound caches almost always have consistency issues, but at least the amount of time that the issue would be present is limited to the expiry time of each entry. However, we must consider the application's access to this data, because if the frequency of accessing a particular entry is less than the cache expiry time of it, the cache is providing no real benefit.

Write through caches are consistent in isolation and can be configured to offer strict consistency, but if multiple write through caches exist within the overall architecture, then there will be consistency issues between them. We can avoid this by having a more intelligent cache, which features a communication mechanism between nodes, that can propagate entry invalidations to each other.

In practice, an ideal cache would feature a combination of both features, so that entries would be held for a known maximum time, but also passes around invalidations as changes are made.

So our evolved architecture would look a bit like the following figure:

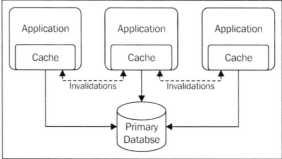

So far we've had a look through the general issues in scaling our data layer, and introduced strategies to help combat the trade-offs we will encounter along the way; however, the real world isn't quite as simple. There are various cache servers and in-memory database products in this area: however, most of these are stand-alone single instances, perhaps with some degree of distribution bolted on or provided by other supporting technologies. This tends to bring about the same issues we experienced with just our primary database, in that we could encounter resource saturation or capacity issues if the product is a single instance, or if the distribution doesn't provide consistency control, perhaps inconsistent data, which might harm our application.

Breaking the mould

Hazelcast is a radical new approach to data, designed from the ground up around distribution. It embraces a new scalable way of thinking; in that data should be shared around for both resilience and performance, while allowing us to configure the trade-offs surrounding consistency as the data requirements dictate.

The first major feature to understand about Hazelcast is its masterless nature; each node is configured to be functionally the same. The oldest node in the cluster is the **de facto leader** and manages the membership, automatically delegating as to which node is responsible for what data. In this way as new nodes join or dropout, the process is repeated and the cluster rebalances accordingly. This makes Hazelcast incredibly simple to get up and running, as the system is self-discovering, self-clustering, and works straight out of the box.

However, the second feature to remember is that we are persisting data entirely in-memory; this makes it incredibly fast but this speed comes at a price. When a node is shutdown, all the data that was held on it is lost. We combat this risk to resilience through replication, by holding enough copies of a piece of data across multiple nodes. In the event of failure, the overall cluster will not suffer any data loss. By default, the standard backup count is 1, so we can immediately enjoy basic resilience. But don't pull the plug on more than one node at a time, until the cluster has reacted to the change in membership and reestablished the appropriate number of backup copies of data.

So when we introduce our new masterless distributed cluster, we get something like the following figure:

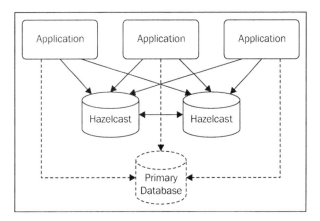

 A distributed cache is by far the most powerful as it can scale up in response to changes in the application's needs.

We previously identified that multi-node caches tend to suffer from either saturation or consistency issues. In the case of Hazelcast, each node is the owner of a number of partitions of the overall data, so the load will be fairly spread across the cluster. Hence, any saturation would be at the cluster level rather than any individual node. We can address this issue simply by adding more nodes. In terms of consistency, by default the backup copies of the data are internal to Hazelcast and not directly used, as such we enjoy strict consistency. This does mean that we have to interact with a specific node to retrieve or update a particular piece of data; however, exactly which node that is an internal operational detail and can vary over time— we as developers never actually need to know.

If we imagine that our data is split into a number of partitions, that each partition slice is owned by one node and backed up on another, we could then visualize the interactions like the following figure:

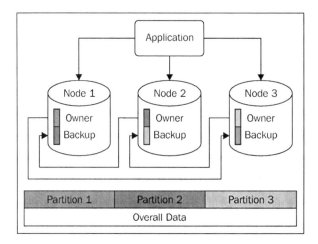

This means that for data belonging to **Partition 1**, our application will have to communicate to **Node 1**, **Node 2** for data belonging to **Partition 2**, and so on. The slicing of the data into each partition is dynamic; so in practice, where there are more partitions than nodes, each node will own a number of different partitions and hold backups for others. As we have mentioned before, all of this is an internal operational detail, and our application does not need to know it, but it is important that we understand what is going on behind the scenes.

Moving to a new ground

So far we have been talking mostly about simple persisted data and caches, but in reality, we should not think of Hazelcast as purely a cache, as it is much more powerful than just that. It is an in-memory data grid that supports a number of distributed collections and features. We can load in data from various sources into differing structures, send messages across the cluster, take out locks to guard against concurrent activity, and listen to the goings on inside the workings of the cluster. Most of these implementations correspond to a standard Java collection, or function in a manner comparable to other similar technologies, but all with the distribution and resilience capabilities already built in.

- Standard utility collections
    - **Map**: Key-value pairs
    - **List**: Collection of objects

- ° **Set**: Non-duplicated collection
- ° **Queue**: Offer/poll FIFO collection
- Specialized collection
  - ° **Multi-Map**: Key-list of values collection
- **Lock**: Cluster wide mutex
- **Topic**: Publish/subscribe messaging
- Concurrency utilities
  - ° **AtomicNumber**: Cluster-wide atomic counter
  - ° **IdGenerator**: Cluster-wide unique identifier generation
  - ° **Semaphore**: Concurrency limitation
  - ° **CountdownLatch**: Concurrent activity gate-keeping
- **Listeners**: Application notifications as things happen

In addition to data storage collections, Hazelcast also features a distributed executor service allowing runnable tasks to be created that can be run anywhere on the cluster to obtain, manipulate, and store results. We could have a number of collections containing source data, then spin up a number of tasks to process the disparate data (for example, averaging or aggregating) and outputting the results into another collection for consumption.

Again, just as we could scale up our data capacities by adding more nodes, we can also increase the execution capacity in exactly the same way. This essentially means that by building our data layer around Hazelcast, if our application needs rapidly increase, we can continuously increase the number of nodes to satisfy seemingly extensive demands, all without having to redesign or re-architect the actual application.

Summary

With Hazelcast, we are dealing more with a technology than a server product, a library to build a system around rather than retrospectively bolting it on, or blindly connecting to an off-the-shelf commercial system. While it is possible (and in some simple cases quite practical) to run Hazelcast as a separate server-like cluster and connect to it remotely from our application, some of the greatest benefits come when we develop our own classes and tasks run within it and alongside it.

With such a large range of generic capabilities, there is an entire world of problems that Hazelcast can help solve. We can use the technology in many ways; in isolation to hold data such as user sessions, run it alongside a more long-term persistent data store to increase capacity, or shift towards performing high performance and scalable operations on our data. By moving more and more responsibility away from monolithic systems to such a generic scalable one, there is no limit to the performance we can unlock.

This will allow us to keep our application and data layers separate, but enabling the ability to scale them up independently as our application grows. This will avoid our application becoming a victim of its own success, while hopefully taking the world by storm.

In the next chapter, we shall start using the technology itself and investigate the data collections we have just discovered.

2
Getting off the Ground

Simply put, we can think of Hazelcast as a library technology — a JAR file that we bring into our application's classpath, and integrate with in order to harness its data distribution capabilities. Now, there are many ways we could go about setting up an application to use various third-party libraries and dependencies. Most modern IDEs can do this for you. Dependency management or build tools such as Maven, Ant, or Gradle can automate it, and we could sort all of it out ourselves manually. But it's now time to jump in, head first into the deep end. In this chapter, we shall:

- Download Hazelcast
- Create a basic application around the technology
- Explore the various simple storage collections
- Fetch and search our stored data
- Set limits and understand what happens when we reach these

Let's get started

First things first, let's create a working directory for our project.

Now, let's navigate to Hazelcast's download page:

`www.hazelcast.com/downloads.jsp`

The following image shows what the downloading page should look like:

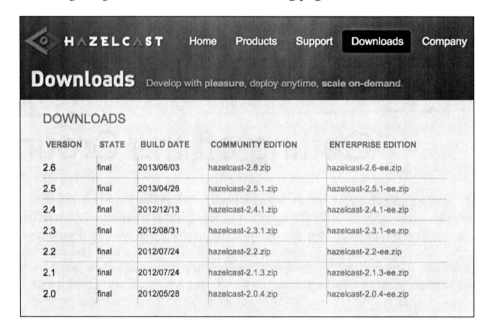

We will use the latest version, in this case Version 2.6.

 While there is nothing stopping you working with the enterprise edition, there is nothing within this book that requires it. For our purposes, the community edition will do just fine.

In unpacking the archive, you will find a lib/ directory. This contains the various library JAR files we could use within our application. For now, let's copy lib/ hazelcast-2.6.jar to our working directory.

Showing off straightaway

Within the Hazelcast JAR, there is the very useful utility class TestApp. The class name is a little deceptive as it can be used in more ways than just testing, but its greatest offering is that it provides a simple text console for easy access to distributed collections.

To fire this up, we need to run this class using the Hazelcast JAR as the classpath.

```
$ java -cp hazelcast-2.6.jar com.hazelcast.examples.TestApp
```

This should bring up a fair amount of verbose logging, but a reassuring section to look for to show that a cluster has been formed is the following code:

```
Members [1] {
    Member [127.0.0.1]:5701 this
}
```

This lets us know that a new cluster of one node has been created with the node indicated by `this`. The configuration that was used to start up this instance is the default one built into the JAR. You can find a copy of it at `bin/hazelcast.xml` from within the unpacked archive that we downloaded in the previous section. We should now be presented with a basic console interface prompt provided by the `TestApp` class.

```
hazelcast[default] >
```

To get lots of information about using the console, issue the `help` command. The response will be quite extensive but will be along the lines of the following command line:

```
hazelcast[default] > help
Commands:
-- General commands
jvm
  //displays info about the runtime
who
  //displays info about the cluster
whoami
  //displays info about this cluster member
ns <string>
  //switch the namespace

-- Map commands
m.put <key> <value>
  //puts an entry to the map
m.remove <key>
  //removes the entry of given key from the map
m.get <key>
  //returns the value of given key from the map
m.keys
  //iterates the keys of the map
m.values
  //iterates the values of the map
```

```
m.entries
  //iterates the entries of the map
m.size
  //size of the map
m.clear
  //clears the map
m.destroy
  //destroys the map
```

We can now use the various map manipulation commands such as `m.put`, `m.get`, and `m.remove` to interact with the default distributed map.

```
hazelcast[default] > m.put foo bar
null

hazelcast[default] > m.get foo
bar

hazelcast[default] > m.entries
foo : bar
Total 1

hazelcast[default] > m.remove foo
bar

hazelcast[default] > m.size
Size = 0
```

Obviously, while our map has the potential of being distributed, as we're only running a single node instance, any changes will be lost when it shuts down. To avoid this, let us start up another node. As each node should be identical in its configuration, let's repeat exactly the same process we used before to start up the first node; however, this time we should see two nodes in the startup logging. This lets us know that our example application has successfully joined the existing cluster created by the `TestApp` console.

```
Members [2] {
    Member [127.0.0.1]:5701
    Member [127.0.0.1]:5702 this
}
```

If you don't see two nodes, it is possible that the network interface that Hazelcast is selecting by default doesn't support multicast. You can further confirm that this is likely to be the case by checking the interface associated with the IP address listed in logging and looking for the following line:

```
WARNING: [127.0.0.1]:5702 [dev] Config seed port is 5701 and cluster size
is 1. Some of the ports seem occupied!
```

To address this, the simplest solution at this stage is to disable the offending interface if you are able to do so. Otherwise, copy the `bin/hazelcast.xml` configuration to our working directory, and edit it to force Hazelcast to a particular network interface like the following one which will definitely fix the issue, but does skip a little further ahead:

```
<interfaces enabled="true">
  <interface>127.0.0.1</interface>
</interfaces>
```

Once we have successfully started the second node, we should immediately have access to the same data that we have persisted on the first. Additionally behind the scenes, Hazelcast will be rebalancing the cluster to take advantage of the new node making it the owner of a number of partitions, as well as creating a backup copy of all the data that is held on both nodes. We should be able to confirm that this is happening by having a closer look at the log entries being generated.

```
INFO: [127.0.0.1]:5701 [dev] Re-partitioning cluster data... Immediate-
Tasks: 271, Scheduled-Tasks: 0
```

Hazelcast can handle new nodes appearing pretty much at any time without risk to its data. We can simulate a node failure by invoking the `exit` command on one of our test console nodes in order to shut it down (*Ctrl + C* also has the same effect). The actual data held on it will be lost, but if we were to restart the node, it should come back with all the previous data. This is because the other node remained running and was able to reinitialize the failed node with the cluster data as it started backup. As we learned in the previous section, by default, the standard backup count is 1 (which we look to configure later on), so as long as we don't have more node failures than the backup count in a short amount of time (before the cluster has had a chance to react and rebalance the data), then we shall not encounter any overall data loss. Why not give this a try, let's see if we can lose some data; after all it's only held in-memory!

One sure-fire way to expose this issue is to create a cluster of many nodes (importantly having more nodes than the backup count) and fail a number of them in quick succession. To try this, we can use the test console to create a map with a large number of entries.

```
hazelcast[default] > m.putmany 10000
size = 10000, 1222 evt/s, 954 Kbit/s, 976 KB added


hazelcast[default] > m.size
Size = 10000
```

Then quickly fail multiple nodes. We should get the following login indicating potential data loss and can confirm the extent of the loss by looking at the size of our map:

```
WARNING: [127.0.0.1]:5701 [dev] Owner of partition is being removed!
Possible data loss for partition[213].


hazelcast[default] > m.size
Size = 8250
```

This tells us that we can add more nodes to a cluster quite quickly without risking the overall data, but we have to allow Hazelcast enough time to rebalance the cluster if we remove nodes. We can see this rebalancing occurring in the logs of the remaining nodes, as partitions owned by the now dead node are reassigned. To find out when things have calmed down, we can use a migration listener to give us more visibility on this process, but that's a topic for later.

```
INFO: [127.0.0.1]:5701 [dev] Re-partitioning cluster data... Immediate-
Tasks: 181, Scheduled-Tasks: 0
```

For the case of failure, we will need to understand our infrastructure's stability, and set the backup count levels high enough to be able to handle a certain amount of the unexpected data.

Downloading the example code

You can download the example code files for all Packt Publishing books you have purchased from your account at http://www.packtpub.com. If you purchased this book elsewhere, you can visit http://www.packtpub.com/support and register to have the files e-mailed directly to you.

Mapping back to the real world

Having briefly explored Hazelcast's distributed capabilities via a test console, let's have a look at how we are more likely to interact with a cluster in the real world. Let's create a new `SimpleMapExample` class with a main method to spin up and manipulate a named distributed map called `capitals`. Hazelcast refers to these named collections as a **namespace** and must be uniquely named across the cluster.

```java
import com.hazelcast.core.Hazelcast;
import com.hazelcast.core.HazelcastInstance;
import java.util.Map;

public class SimpleMapExample {
  public static void main(String[] args) {
    HazelcastInstance hz = Hazelcast.newHazelcastInstance();

    Map<String, String> capitals = hz.getMap("capitals");
    capitals.put("GB", "London");
    capitals.put("FR", "Paris");
    capitals.put("US", "Washington DC");
    capitals.put("AU", "Canberra");

    System.err.println(
      "Known capital cities: " + capitals.size());

    System.err.println(
      "Capital city of GB: " + capitals.get("GB"));
  }
}
```

As before, we should see various logging entries on the startup as well as the fun fact outputs; confirming we persisted into and retrieved from the map programmatically. We can also use this example in conjunction with our `TestApp` console from the previous section and interact with the new map `capitals`. To do this, we will need to switch namespaces from within the console before interacting with the map. Remember to make sure they have formed a cluster when using the console if you closed it since the previous example.

```
hazelcast[default] > ns capitals
namespace: capitals


hazelcast[capitals] > m.get GB
London
```

As with other implementations of Java maps, if we are creating our own objects for use within a Hazelcast map, we will need to consider the use of the custom equals() and hashCode() methods; however, it is the serialized binary form of the object that is used instead of these custom methods when the object is used as a key to a Hazelcast map entry.

Sets, lists, and queues

In our previous examples, we have looked at key/value storage provided by Hazelcast maps; however, there are a number of other collections that provide keyless groups of objects. Two of these additional types are distributed versions of collections that we are hopefully already familiar with—sets and lists.

As we know, the primary difference between the two is that lists allow for multiple entries and a set does not. So if we add them to our previous map example, we get the following code:

```
Set<String> cities = hz.getSet("cities");
cities.addAll(captials.values());
cities.add("London");
cities.add("Rome");
cities.add("New York");

List<String> countries = hz.getList("countries");
countries.addAll(captials.keySet());
countries.add("CA");
countries.add("DE");
countries.add("GB"); // duplicate entry
```

In using our test console again to interact with these new collections, we will have to use different commands as we are now interacting with a set and a list rather than a map. You can refer to the help response for further options, but s.iterator and l.iterator will print out the contents of each for sets and lists respectively.

```
hazelcast[default] > ns cities
namespace: cities

hazelcast[cities] > s.iterator
1 London
2 New York
3 Paris
4 Rome
5 Washington DC
```

```
6 Canberra

hazelcast[cities] > ns countries
namespace: countries

hazelcast[countries] > l.iterator
1 FR
2 AU
3 US
4 GB
5 CA
6 DE
7 GB
```

The last of the generic storage collections that Hazelcast provides is a **first-in first-out (FIFO)** based queue. This provides us with a mechanism to offer objects onto the top of a queue before retrieving them off the bottom. Such a structure would be incredibly useful if we had a number of tasks to individually handle by a number of client workers.

Let create a new `SimpleQueueExample` class again with a main method, but this time we're going to create an iterator to continuously handle objects taken from the queue.

```
import com.hazelcast.core.Hazelcast;
import com.hazelcast.core.HazelcastInstance;

import java.util.concurrent.BlockingQueue;

public class SimpleQueueExample {
  public static void main(String[] args) throws Exception {
    HazelcastInstance hz = Hazelcast.newHazelcastInstance();

    BlockingQueue<String> arrivals = hz.getQueue("arrivals");

    while (true) {
      String arrival = arrivals.take();

      System.err.println(
        "New arrival from: " + arrival);
    }
  }
}
```

Like before, we can use our test console to interact with the queue. This time we can offer items to the queue for our client to take and print out. A FIFO queue should only provide an individual item to a single consumer irrespective of the number of consumers connected to the queue. We can validate that Hazelcast is honoring this behavior by running our example client multiple times.

```
hazelcast[default] > ns arrivals
namespace: arrivals
hazelcast[default] > q.offer Heathrow
true

hazelcast[arrivals] > q.offer JFK
true
```

From the output of our `SimpleQueueExample` client, we should then be able to see the following messages. If we are running multiple clients by this point, then the output will be spread between them and certainly not duplicated.

```
New arrival from: Heathrow

New arrival from: JFK
```

As we mentioned before, queues are great for providing a single pipeline for work distribution. Items can be concurrently offered onto it before being taken off in parallel by workers. With Hazelcast ensuring that each item is only reliably delivered to a single worker while providing us with the distribution, resilience and scalability are not present when comparing the alternative queuing systems.

Many things at a time

We have seen previously that Hazelcast provides us with a generic key/value map; however, one popular use of this capability would be to create a key/list-of-values map. While there is nothing stopping us from defining these ourselves using standard Java generics, we will have to manually handle the initialization of each key entry. Hazelcast has luckily gone out of its way to make our lives easier by handling this case for us, through the use of the specialized `MultiMap` collection.

Let's have a look at the following example:

```java
Map<String, List<String>> manualCities = hz.getMap("manualCities");

List<String> gbCities = new ArrayList<String>();
manualCities.put("GB", gbCities);
```

```
gbCities = manualCities.get("GB");
gbCities.add("London");
manualCities.put("GB", gbCities);

gbCities = manualCities.get("GB");
gbCities.add("Southampton");
manualCities.put("GB", gbCities);

List<String> frCities = new ArrayList<String>();
manualCities.put("FR", frCities);

frCities = manualCities.get("FR");
manualCities.get("FR").add("Paris");
manualCities.put("FR", frCities);

System.err.println(
  String.format("Manual: GB=%s, FR=%s",
    manualCities.get("GB"),
    manualCities.get("FR")));


MultiMap<String, String> multiMapCities =
  hz.getMultiMap("multiMapCities");

multiMapCities.put("GB", "London");
multiMapCities.put("GB", "Southampton");

multiMapCities.put("FR", "Paris");

System.err.println(
  String.format("MultiMap: GB=%s, FR=%s",
    multiMapCities.get("GB"),
    multiMapCities.get("FR")));
```

As we can clearly see, the use of MultiMap in this way dramatically simplifies the code as well as allowing you to modify the underlying map using delta changes rather than having to fully retrieve, modify, and persist for what could be a small change in a large list. One important point to be aware of is that we can't use a Hazelcast map in a pass-by-reference context, as we might do with a native Java implementation. For example, the following optimization of the previous code would not achieve the desired result:

```
manualCities.get("GB").put("Leeds");
```

This is because Hazelcast always returns a cloned copy of the data rather than the instance actually held; so modifying the returned object as we would in the preceding code does not actually update the persisted value.

Searching and indexing

In moving towards creating clean key/value-based storage, we may find that we have lost some of the extra searching capabilities that traditional databases offer. Mainly that we now can't find records within a dataset without knowing the primary key to that entry. However, fear not, as Hazelcast provides similar capabilities for searching its maps by predefined indexes. These can be either ordered (ascending) or unordered, depending on our particular data needs. But be aware that indexing doesn't come for free; the internal lookup table used to provide the quick searching on reads is maintained as we make changes to the map; this will add latency to every write operation to that namespace.

So firstly, let's create a new **plain old Java object (POJO)** to represent a city.

```java
import java.io.Serializable;

public class City implements Serializable {
  private String name;
  private String country;
  private int population;

  public City(String name, String country, int population) {
    this.name = name;
    this.country = country;
    this.population = population;
  }

  public String getName() {
    return name;
  }

  public void setName(String name) {
    this.name = name;
  }

  public String getCountry() {
    return country;
  }

  public void setCountry(String country) {
```

```
    this.country = country;
  }

  public int getPopulation() {
    return population;
  }

  public void setPopulation(int population) {
    this.population = population;
  }

  @Override
  public boolean equals(Object o) {
    if (this == o) return true;
    if (o == null || getClass() != o.getClass()) return false;
    City other = (City) o;
    if (!this.country.equals(other.country)) return false;
    if (!this.name.equals(other.name)) return false;

    return true;
  }

  @Override
  public int hashCode() {
    int result = name.hashCode();
    result = 31 * result + country.hashCode();
    return result;
  }

  @Override
  public String toString() {
    return String.format(
      "City{name='%s', country='%s', population=%d}",
      name, country, population);
  }
}
```

As you can see, we have created our `City` class to implement `Serializable` so that it can be correctly persisted within Hazelcast. We have also implemented the `equals()` and `hashCode()` methods so the required behavior is ensured. Additionally, a `toString()` method has been added for debugging convenience.

Using this, we can update our previous map example to use our new city POJO. One major change from the previous example is that in order to access the additional indexing functionally, we have to use the Hazelcast specific IMap interface rather than the standard Java Map that we used before.

In order to search the map, we need to provide a Predicate object to filter on. One such implementation of this is that we can use SqlPredicate, which provides us with the ability to use a SQL-like syntax to describe the filter.

```
IMap<String, City> capitals = hz.getMap("capitals");
capitals.addIndex("name", false);
capitals.addIndex("population", true);

capitals.put("GB",
  new City("London", "GB", 8174100));

capitals.put("FR",
  new City("Paris", "FR", 2268265));

capitals.put("US",
  new City("Washington DC", "US", 601723));

capitals.put("AU",
  new City("Canberra", "AU", 354644));

Collection<City> possibleLondons = capitals.values(
  new SqlPredicate("name = 'London'")););

System.err.println(possibleLondons);


Collection<City> largeCities = capitals.values(
  new SqlPredicate("population > 1000000"));

System.err.println(largeCities);
```

The supported syntax is very much a limited subset of SQL, but should feel familiar.

- **AND/OR**: For combining multiple expressions
- **=, !=, <, <=, >, >=**: For expression comparison
- **LIKE**: For simple string pattern matching expressions
- **IN**: For providing a defined list of sought values
- **BETWEEN**: For providing a range of sought numeric values
- **NOT**: Can be used as a prefix to negate the expression

The preceding functions are used in the following code:

```
country = 'GB' AND population BETWEEN 10000 AND 100000

country NOT IN ('GB', 'FR')

name LIKE 'L%'
```

If you would prefer to construct your query more programmatically, we can use a JPA-like criteria API provided by `PredicateBuilder`, or more manually using various helper methods in `Predicates`. We could use the following alternative code in place of our previous SQL based predicates:

```
EntryObject c = new PredicateBuilder().getEntryObject();
Predicate londonPredicate = c.get("name").equal("London");

Collection<City> possibleLondons = capitals.values(londonPredicate);

System.err.println(possibleLondons);


Predicate largeCityPredicate = Predicates.greaterThan(
  Predicates.get("population"), 1000000);

Collection<City> largeCities = capitals.values(largeCityPredicate);

System.err.println(largeCities);
```

What happens when we reach our limits?

As large as we may scale our cluster to handle ever-growing datasets, it is quite possible that we will want to configure a map to feature specific behavior. The main things we can customize the number of backup counts and types, limits on how big a particular map can grow plus what we do when we reach that limit, and defining a default lifespan for our entries. We can use the `hazelcast.xml` configuration to define this behavior for all maps or for an individual one. Now, we can copy the configuration from the unpacked download `bin/hazelcast.xml` to our working directory, and add a custom configuration for our `capitals` map.

```
<map name="capitals">

  <max-size policy="cluster_wide_map_size">10</max-size>
  <eviction-policy>LFU</eviction-policy>
  <eviction-percentage>20</eviction-percentage>
```

```
<backup-count>1</backup-count>
<async-backup-count>1</async-backup-count>

<time-to-live-seconds>86400</time-to-live-seconds>
<max-idle-seconds>3600</max-idle-seconds>

</map>
```

The properties we have put in place should all be relatively self-explanatory, but let's go through them in a little more detail as there are a few that demand closer inspection.

The first set deals with bounding the size of the map and what to do when that limit is reached.

The max-size parameter as you would expect governs how big a map may grow before we have a clear out and evict existing entries for make room to potential future ones. However, we can additionally pick from five different types of policies to vary this behavior.

The first (and the default) policy is the easiest to understand.

- cluster_wide_map_size
    - Maximum number of entries across the entire cluster

The second one is probably the least useful in a real world scenario.

- partitions_wide_map_size
    - Maximum number of entries per internal partition slice
    - The number of partitions is also configurable, but as a cluster-wide parameter rather than specific to any one map

The latter three policies relate to the usage on an individual node basis.

- max_size_per_jvm
    - Maximum number of entries per node

- used_heap_size
    - Maximum heap usage in megabytes

- used_heap_percentage
    - Maximum proportion of the total heap size

eviction-policy governs the strategy used to select entries to discard when making room for new ones; there are few options to pick from.

- **NONE**
  - ○ No eviction (default)
- **Least Recently Used (LRU)**
  - ○ The oldest interacted with the entries
- **Least Frequency Used (LFU)**
  - ○ The least interacted with the entries

eviction-percentage dictates when we trigger an eviction, and how much space we preemptively need to create relative to the overall max-size of the map.

The next set of configurations deal with backup copies of entries both in terms of number of duplicate copies to hold, but also the method and consistency of how they are created.

- backup-count controls the number of backup copies created synchronously on each change. Increasing this number significantly will have performance implications as we will have to block waiting upon confirmations this many nodes.
- async-backup-count controls the number of backup copies that are created asynchronously on a best effort basis. This figure combined with backup-count determines the total number of backup copies to be held.

The final set is used to set a map-wide default TTL for entries.

- time-to-live-seconds is a default dumb TTL for each entry. Entities will be removed from the map after this amount of time, irrespective of use or resetting when overwritten.
- max-idle-seconds sets the maximum time that an entry can sit unused before being expired.

Summary

One of Hazelcast's greatest strengths is the ease of getting going with neighbor self-discovery and automatic clustering we can create a basic resilience and consistent data source in minutes. While there is plenty of detail left to cover and simple examples don't paint a full picture, we have hopefully already gained a lot of confidence in the technology. As we move forward, we will explore the increasing specialized functionality and understand your application's individual needs that will dictate how valuable each topic is to you.

In the next chapter, we shall move on a little further, starting to use the more concurrent capabilities on offer.

3
Going Concurrent

Along with the simple distributed collections offered, Hazelcast also provides us with additional complementary capabilities, allowing us to further parallelize our applications. Some of these features come as standard within more traditional data stores, while others are inspired by similar technologies. In this chapter we will look at:

- Atomic and consistent nature of simple collections
- Distributed locking to provide a cluster wide mutex
- Transactional support to cater for more complex operations
- Cluster-wide atomic ID generator
- JMS-like topics for broadcast messaging (publish, subscribe)

Atomic control

When interacting with Hazelcast's distributed collections, we set and retrieve data in a consistent and atomic way. In that when we modify an entry, it is immediately available on other nodes irrespective of their processing state. This does mean that we have to be careful when developing our applications, as data may change underneath us while performing an operation. However, it is this default lockless nature that significantly increases application scalability, especially under load. Two of the collections we have previously looked at additionally implement specific atomic capabilities provided by the `java.util.concurrent` interfaces.

As we've previously seen, the distributed map collection provided by Hazelcast is defined by its own `IMap` class. This actually extends `ConcurrentMap`, which will provide us with additional atomic operations such as `putIfAbsent(key, value)` and `replace(key, oldValue, newValue)`. These capabilities may go some way to prevent any concurrent modification, as we are able to detect when a change has occurred, and handle it appropriately within the application layer.

We can see how we might use this behavior in the following code:

```
public class AtomicMapExample {
  public static void main(String[] args) {
    HazelcastInstance hz = Hazelcast.newHazelcastInstance();

    IMap<String, String> capitals = hz.getMap("capitals");

    capitals.putIfAbsent("GB", "Winchester");
    System.err.println("Capital of GB (until 1066): " +
      capitals.get("GB"));

    String actualCapital = capitals.putIfAbsent("GB", "London");
    System.err.println
      ("Failed to put as already present: " +
      capitals.get("GB") + " = " + actualCapital);

    boolean r1 = capitals.replace("GB", "Southampton", "London");
    System.err.println("Failed to replace as incorrect old value: " +
      capitals.get("GB") + "; [" + r1 + "]");

    boolean r2 = capitals.replace("GB", "Winchester", "London");
    System.err.println("Capital of GB (since 1066): " +
      capitals.get("GB") + "; [" + r2 + "]");
  }
}
```

Another collection we've worked with so far is the distributed queues. Like their map counterparts they are also specialized, this time by the IQueue interface; in this case extending the BlockingQueue concurrency features. The additional features offering allows us to control how our application reacts to the pushing and popping of the FIFO queue, in using the various add(item), offer(item), and put(item) methods, to push onto the queue depending on whether we wish to throw an exception, return a success, or block. For retrieval, we can use poll() and take() for instant access, blocking, or waiting for an item to be available. However, indefinitely blocking can be problematic; the offer(item) and poll() methods can optionally take a defined timeout, allowing our application to fail more gracefully if the attempted operation cannot be completed within the specified time.

Distributed locking

In building a broad scalable application, one aspect we tend to lose is our ability to restrict and prevent concurrent activity. Within a single JVM we would use a synchronized lock to gatekeeper, a section of functionality from concurrent execution. Once we move away from a single JVM, this problem becomes a much bigger issue. Traditional approaches would leverage a transactional database to provide a system for locking, in the form of a table rowlock or transactional state. However, this approach presents us with a single point of failure and concurrency issues when scaling up our application.

Hazelcast offers a distributed locking facility, allowing us to attempt to acquire a cluster-wide named lock and to gatekeeper the functionality behind it. If we can create an example class LockingExample, we can demonstrate this ability.

```java
public class LockingExample {
  public static void main(String[] args) throws Exception {
    HazelcastInstance hz = Hazelcast.newHazelcastInstance();

    Lock lock = hz.getLock("theTime");

    while (true) {
      if (lock.tryLock(30, TimeUnit.SECONDS)) {
        try {
          while (true) {
            System.err.println(new Date());
            Thread.sleep(1000);
          }
        }
        finally {
          lock.unlock();
        }
      }
    }
  }
}
```

In considering the preceding code, we are continuously attempting to acquire the Time lock. Should we be successful in acquiring the lock, we shall start continuously printing out the time every second. In running our class once, we will see the behavior as described.

```
Members [1] {
  Member [127.0.0.1]:5701 this
}

Tue Jan 01 00:00:00 UTC 2013
Tue Jan 01 00:00:01 UTC 2013
Tue Jan 01 00:00:02 UTC 2013
Tue Jan 01 00:00:03 UTC 2013
```

However, once we start running our example multiple times, we have enabled resilience of the locked section. In that, multiple nodes are all continuously trying to enter that block of code, but are prevented by the acquired lock of another code. This is where the locking capability comes into its own; if we were to start killing off nodes, especially the one currently holding the lock, we fail-safe. In killing nodes not holding the lock, the correct behavior is still enforced, but should we kill off the node currently holding the lock, it will be automatically released, as the owner is now dead. At this point another node can now acquire the lock and can take over the responsibility of telling us the time.

Using this capability, we have provided our application with the ability to have a resilient but exclusive execution task that exists within the cluster. Where that task actually occurs isn't particularly controllable; but assuming nodes are present, it is guaranteed to run somewhere, but only once.

Tactical locking

In addition to a single blunt gatekeeper locking where we effectively prevent concurrent execution across the entire cluster for a specific type of activity, we might want to lock on a more specific context. Rather than using a Lock object, IMap provides us with key locking capabilities. Using this, we can acquire a mutex on a specific entry, enabling the ability to prevent concurrent modifications on a targeted piece of data.

```
public class MapLockingExample {
  public static void main(String[] args) {
    HazelcastInstance hz = Hazelcast.newHazelcastInstance();

    IMap<String, Date> arrivals = hz.getMap("arrivals");

    if (arrivals.tryLock("London")) {
      try {
        arrivals.put("London", new Date());
      }
      finally {
        arrivals.unlock("London");
      }
    }
  }
}
```

While we have explicitly acquired, processed, and reliably released the lock, this gives us absolute control over the amount of blocking we might be introducing into our application; if used wisely this is a very powerful tool.

Transactionally rolling on

Now that we have looked at the simple atomic approach we can take when dealing with the concurrency of consumption and changes to the persisted data, what happens if this is just too simple for our use case? Well, now that we have the ability to lock both globally across the cluster and on individual data items, we can prevent unexpected changes to our supporting data in the middle of an operation. But if we needed to stop and undo changes we had made part way through an operation, how might we achieve that?

Luckily, drawing on inspiration from traditional roots, Hazelcast provides us with transactional capabilities. Offering a REPEATABLE_READ transaction isolation (the only transactional mode currently supported), once you enter a transaction, Hazelcast will automatically acquire the appropriate key locks for each entry that is interacted with; any changes we write will be buffered locally until the transaction is complete. If the transaction was successful and was committed, all the locally buffered changes will be flushed out to the wider cluster, and the locks released. If the transaction was rolled back, we simply release our locks without flushing out the local changes.

Look at the following example:

```java
public class TransactionExample {
  public static void main(String[] args) throws Exception {
    HazelcastInstance hz = Hazelcast.newHazelcastInstance();

    Map<String, String> testMap = hz.getMap("test");

    Transaction tx = hz.getTransaction();
    tx.begin();

    try {
      System.err.println(testMap.get("foo"));

      Thread.sleep(30000);

      System.err.println(testMap.get("foo"));
      testMap.put("foo", "bar");

      tx.commit();
    }
    catch (Exception e) {
      tx.rollback();
    }
  }
}
```

If we fire up our `TestApp` console from earlier and attempt to manipulate the `test` map during our 30 second pause interacting with keys other than `foo` will succeed as normal, however, while we can read from `foo`, writing to it will cause our console to block until our application completes its transaction. So from our `TransactionExample` application, we will consistently see:

```
Members [2] {
  Member [127.0.0.1]:5701 this
  Member [127.0.0.1]:5702
}


null
null
```

Despite our best efforts from the `TestApp` console to disrupt that functionality:

```
Members [2] {
  Member [127.0.0.1]:5701
  Member [127.0.0.1]:5702 this
}

hazelcast[test] > m.put other wibble
null

hazelcast[test] > m.get other
wibble

hazelcast[test] > m.get foo
null

hazelcast[test] > m.put foo chew
<blocked until transaction completes>
bar
```

We can see the process of what is going on under the hood in the following diagram:

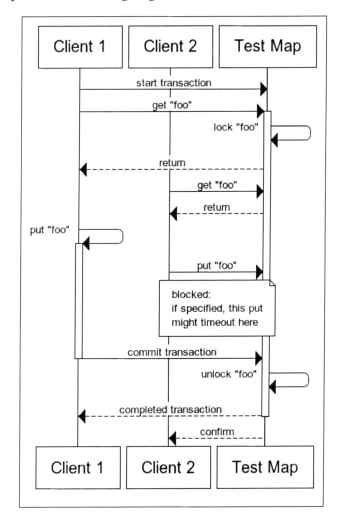

Differences when queuing

Unlike the storage collections where the transactional nature is when writing, hence able to be buffered locally before flushing on commit, queues are transactional on reads. This is as if we were to take an item from the queue and then roll back, the item would need to be returned to the queue so it could be redelivered; but what if our node died within the transaction— it wouldn't be able to return it. To avoid this situation rather than buffering locally, taken values are copied to the next node in the cluster to be buffered remotely. That way should the node disappear, another node is in a position to restore the rolled back item to the queue.

Enterprising onwards

If we are going to use Hazelcast within an enterprise J2EE container, we can also integrate this provided transaction support as a standard resource adapter. While the details will vary depending on the container you are using, it would be best to follow any relevant documentation you have for your specific case, the required `hazelcast-ra-2.6.rar` file can be found in the `lib/` directory of our previously downloaded archive.

Collectively counting up

Another piece of functionality we have lost in migrating away from a traditional data source is our ability to generate a sequence number or an autogenerated identifier. One primary issue with the original mechanism is the single point of failure in our previous data source. Hazelcast fortunately provides us with a distributed alternative in the form of `IdGenerator`.

This instance provides us with a cluster-wide unique identifier generator from which we can request a new unique identifier to be issued. We have to be aware that the internal counter state is only persisted during the life span of the cluster; should all the nodes be lost, the counter will restart at zero. Let's consider the following `IdGeneratorExample` code:

```
public class IdGeneratorExample {
  public static void main(String[] args) throws Exception {
    HazelcastInstance hz = Hazelcast.newHazelcastInstance();

    IdGenerator idGen = hz.getIdGenerator("newId");

    while (true) {
      Long id = idGen.newId();
      System.err.println("New Id: " + id);
      Thread.sleep(1000);
    }
  }
}
```

In running this multiple times, we will see that the generated values are unique and counting upwards within their own group of identifiers.

```
Members [1] {
  Member [127.0.0.1]:5701 this
}
```

```
New Id: 1
New Id: 2
New Id: 3


Members [2] {
  Member [127.0.0.1]:5701
  Member [127.0.0.1]:5702 this
}

New Id: 1000001
New Id: 1000002
New Id: 1000003
```

As you can probably tell from the output, groups of 1 million are allocated to each node to start with. Once that pool of identifiers has been exhausted, a new pool of 1 million is allocated. This process is repeated as much as required, with possible values starting from zero and the largest value that can be issued being Long.MAX_VALUE.

Spreading the word

The final collection capability offered by Hazelcast is a broadcast messaging system. This is very much inspired by JMS topics and offers a comparable set of features, in that, we can publish events on to messaging bus to deliver to a large number of subscribed receivers.

As we can see in the following diagram, an application can publish a message onto a topic that will then be distributed across over to all instances of our application who have subscribed to the topic. This will include the instance that originally sent the message in the first place, assuming it too has a listener subscribed to the topic.

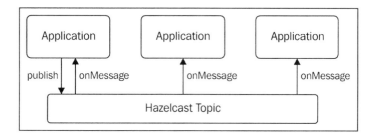

First things first, we'll need a `MessageListener` class to handle messages, implementing an `onMessage(Message<T>)` method as required.

```
public class TopicListener implements MessageListener<String> {

  @Override
  public void onMessage(Message<String> msg) {
    System.err.println("Received: " + msg.getMessageObject());
  }
}
```

Let's create a class to broadcast some messages and register our `TopicListener` class against the broadcast topic, so that each node is advertising itself and with every node hearing everything from all the peer nodes.

```
public class TopicExample {
  public static void main(String[] args) throws Exception {
    HazelcastInstance hz = Hazelcast.newHazelcastInstance();

    ITopic<String> broadcastTopic = hz.getTopic("broadcast");
    broadcastTopic.addMessageListener(new TopicListener());

    while (true) {
      broadcastTopic.publish(
        new Date() + " - " +
        hz.getCluster().getLocalMember() + " says hello");

      Thread.sleep(1000);
    }
  }
}
```

In running our `TopicExample` class multiple times, we'll see all the broadcasts on every node instance.

```
Received: Tue Jan 01 00:00:00 UTC 2013 - Member [127.0.01]:5701 this
says hello
Received: Tue Jan 01 00:00:00 UTC 2013 - Member [127.0.01]:5702 this
says hello

Received: Tue Jan 01 00:00:01 UTC 2013 - Member [127.0.01]:5701 this
says hello
Received: Tue Jan 01 00:00:01 UTC 2013 - Member [127.0.01]:5702 this
says hello
```

One very important thing to be aware of is that the invocation of each listener's onMessage method to deliver the topic message is single threaded; this ensures that messages are received in the same order as the original sender; however, the ordering of messages received from multiple senders is not guaranteed. As we have only one receiving thread, we need to ensure that we don't undergo too complex, lengthy, or blocking an operation method directly within that thread, as we will prevent the delivery of other pending messages. If we do have to perform operations of that nature, our best bet is to spin them out into a local executor to handle. However do remember that once a message has been delivered and passed on to the local executors job queue, it will be vulnerable to be lost should that JVM shutdown uncleanly prior to execution.

```java
public class TopicExecListener implements MessageListener<String> {

    private ExecutorService exec = Executors.newFixedThreadPool(10);

    @Override
    public void onMessage(final Message<String> msg) {
      exec.execute(new Runnable() {

        @Override
        public void run() {
          System.err.println("Received: " + msg.getMessageObject());
        }
      });
    }
}
```

We can see how this decoupling can provide a more timely and reliable delivery of messages from the topic to the application in the following diagram:

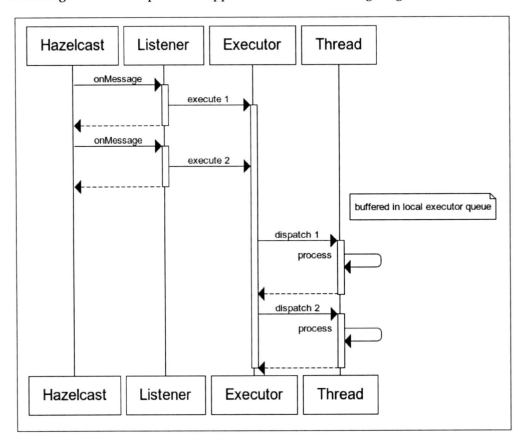

One of the primary benefits on this offering which very much highlights the distributed benefits of Hazelcast, is the lack of any single point of failure; something that is not easily achievable with most other available pure JMS solutions. If we run Hazelcast on multiple nodes and push messages onto a topic, we can enjoy the same level of resilience of our message in terms of persistence that we enjoy with our other collections.

Summary

We have now expanded our awareness of all the data storage and distribution collections offered by Hazelcast. Additionally we have learned about the default atomic nature of data concurrency but also the mechanisms to combat, and gatekeeper concurrency, should our application demand great degrees of control over the data flow. Finally, we have discovered comparable versions of features found in traditional alternatives, as well as offered by other Java technologies. By now we are finding out how extensive and flexible Hazelcast can be. While we've now touched on most of the basics, there is plenty more detail left to be discovered.

Now we have discovered the various types of collections that we have available for us to use in our applications, in the next chapter we shall look at how Hazelcast splits and shares the data around to unlock its incredible scalability.

4
Divide and Conquer

One of the primary advantages of technologies like Hazelcast is the distributed nature of their data persistence; by fragmenting and scattering the held data across many diverse nodes we can achieve high levels of reliability, scalability, and performance. In this chapter we will investigate:

- How data is split into partitions
- How that data is backed up within the overall cluster
- Replicating backups; synchronous versus asynchronous
- Trade-off between read performance and consistency
- How to silo groups of nodes together
- How we can manage network partitioning (split brain syndrome)

Divvying up the data

In order to be resilient, Hazelcast apportions the overall data into slices referred to as partitions, and spreads these across our cluster. To do this, it uses a consistent hashing algorithm on the data keys to consistently assign a piece of data to a particular partition, before assigning the ownership of an entire partition to a particular node. By default there are 271 partitions, however this is configurable using the `hazelcast.map.partition.count` property.

This process allows for transparent and automatic fragmentation of our data, but with tunable behavior, while allowing us to ensure that any shared risks (such as nodes running on the same hardware or sharing the same data center rack) are militated against.

We can visualize the partitioning process in the following diagram:

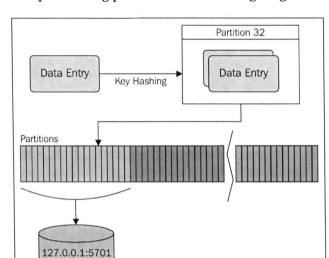

Backups everywhere and nowhere

As each node could disappear or be destroyed at any time without notice; in order to preserve the integrity of the overall persisted data, each partition is backed up on a number of other nodes and must be nodes other than the owner; an individual node can only hold each partition just once (either owning or backing up). Should a node die, the ownership of any partitions that were owned by the now defunct node will be migrated to one of the backups so that no apparent data loss is experienced. Additionally in the background, Hazelcast will start to replicate the migrated partitions over to another node to cater for the fact that there are now fewer backups available than was configured. This will restore resilience back to as it was configured. The number of backups that Hazelcast will create is configurable depending on your hardware's stability, appetite for risk, and available memory.

We can configure the number of backups to keep the method of creation; either globally using the default collection definition, on a per collection basis by explicitly listing the collection name, or using a single wildcard to match against multiple collections simultaneously.

```
<hazelcast>

  <map name="default">
    <backup-count>1</backup-count>
    <async-backup-count>1</async-backup-count>
```

```
        <read-backup-data>false</read-backup-data>
    </map>

    <map name="capitals">
        <backup-count>2</backup-count>
        <async-backup-count>1</async-backup-count>
        <read-backup-data>true</read-backup-data>
    </map>

    <map name="countries.*">
        <backup-count>1</backup-count>
        <async-backup-count>1</async-backup-count>
        <read-backup-data>false</read-backup-data>
    </map>

</hazelcast>
```

backup-count configures the number of backups to keep synchronously up-to-date. This means any manipulation operations (put, delete, and so on) will block until this many configured backups have been notified and have confirmed the change.

async-backup-count specifies the number of backups that will be maintained in the background. The creation of these backups will not block when creating or changing data, but will be replicated out to other nodes on a best effort basis asynchronously by Hazelcast.

The number of copies of data will be governed by these two figures:

```
number-of-copies = 1 owner + backup-count + async-backup-count
```

As we've seen before, by default the backed up copies are there solely for Hazelcast's own internal use and not for direct application use; however, if we wish to expose these backup copies we can do so.

read-backup-data flags that for read operations from this collection we will allow our application to use a backup copy if it is holding a backup of the appropriate partition. This has significant performance benefits as now we can obtain data from a larger number of nodes for a specific piece of data rather than just the owner. However, using this capability in conjunction with a positive async-backup-count, we will introduce the possibility of inconsistent reads. This is as the best effort replication process may not have updated the new data across to the backup before we attempt to read from it. If our application can tolerate this possibility, then we can greatly reduce write latencies (by not blocking on changes) while increasing read performance, but must be used with great care.

Scaling up the cluster

Now that we have created a cluster to house all our data, with a number of nodes holding both owned partitions and backups; but what happens if we need to scale? This could be for a number of reasons, for example, approaching the current memory capacity or our application is rather demanding and saturating a hardware resource. The solution in both cases is simple; add more nodes.

So if we were to start with a cluster of four nodes holding overall 4 million objects, each individual node would hold roughly 1 million owned objects (and a further 1 million backups). When we introduce a new node, Hazelcast reacts by assigning partitions from existing nodes to it. This will cause existing data to stream across to the new node taking on more and more partitions until it holds an overall fair share. The net result will be that each node now only holds approximately 8,00,000 owned objects (and a similar number of backups). In adding this new node we have created additional capacity within the cluster; both in terms of memory and hardware resources.

We previously learned that by default there are 271 partitions, which is a prime number. If we have scaled up our cluster to contain a large number of nodes (anything approaching or above 100), then each node won't own that many partitions and odds are each one is storing a large amount of data. In this situation it would be a good idea to increase the number of partitions, so that the overall data distribution across the cluster is likely to be fairer, and the individual cost of a partition migrating is lower; as moving each one involves less data. This will also reduce the latency of writes during a migration, as these are blocked while the corresponding partition is migrated.

Once the partition ownership has stabilized given the new nodes, it will remain static until something changes; either having another new node joining or if an existing node dies.

Grouping and separating nodes

By default Hazelcast treats each instance as a completely separate node and as such will use any combination of the cluster nodes to hold copies (either for ownership or backups). This instantly introduces a problem where we run multiple JVM instances on the same machine (either physical or virtual). In that any host or hardware level issues that affect one JVM, might affect multiple at the same time, putting data resilience at risk.

To avoid this, we can configure Hazelcast to assign partitions not to an individual node, but to a defined group of nodes. Typically these groups of nodes will be known to share a common external risk or need to balance any differences in available memory; this siloing of nodes is referred to as partition grouping. There are currently two ways to configure a partition group:

Firstly, there exists an automatic process that handles the case of having multiple JVM instances running on the same machine; this is detected by having different nodes sharing the same IP address or interface.

```
<hazelcast>
  <partition-group enabled="true" group-type="HOST_AWARE" />
</hazelcast>
```

The second is a fully manual option which allows us to specify the IP address ranges of the nodes to separate into groupings; while much more complex to configure, allows us to translate more detailed external information that wouldn't otherwise be visible to Hazelcast. For example, allowing us to separate instances running on virtualized hardware than share a common host, hosts that share a common data center rack or any other significant shared risk to which we wish to explicitly cater for the possibility of simultaneous failure of multiple nodes.

```
<hazelcast>
  <partition-group enabled="true" group-type="CUSTOM">

    <member-group>
      <interface>10.0.1.*</interface>
      <interface>10.0.2.1-127</interface>
    </member-group>

    <member-group>
      <interface>10.0.2.128-254</interface>
      <interface>10.0.3.*</interface>
    </member-group>

    <member-group>
      <interface>10.0.4.*</interface>
    </member-group>

  </partition-group>
</hazelcast>
```

One thing to remember either in terms of the default behavior or when using partition groups, if there are fewer destinations for a partition to be assigned to for backups, then we won't be able to satisfy the configured levels of backup counts. To address this we will need to create more nodes or partition groups to accommodate the desired configuration. When using partition groups, what is? is the group that now can only hold one copy of the partition rather than the individual node. So we cannot make a partition group excessively broad, as we may not be able to accommodate the required levels of resilience.

Network partitioning

We have seen that Hazelcast is capable of handling individual node outages, reacting to restore resilience where possible. However it's not just node failures that we have to be able to handle; it could also easily be an issue in the underlying network fabric that can lead to a situation know as split brain syndrome. As this happens away from our application, more at the infrastructure layer, there is very little we can do to prevent it from happening. But we should understand how the problem could affect our application and how the issue is handled when the underlying outage is resolved.

The primary issue for our application is where two (or more) sides of a network outage are able to operate perfectly in isolation. In theory, assuming there were backup copies of the data held on both sides of the split, we will continue to operate normally as two independent deployments. But what happens when the sides become visible again to each other, especially in the case where conflicting changes have occurred? To address this problem, we can define a **merge policy** to govern how to resolve any conflicts.

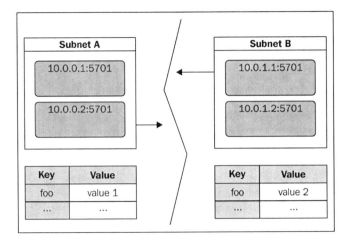

As the value of the `foo` entry differs on either side of the split, when the two sides encounter each other, the oldest node of the cluster will coordinate a merge, establishing which side of the split to merge from and to. This would typically be the smaller side of the split which will merge into the large side; if the two sides are balanced then a hashing algorithm will govern the order. Once this is established, each node of the target side of the merge will sequentially disconnect and reconnect to the cluster, sending a merge request for each entry it previously held using a merge policy to determine whether to retain or override.

Merge policies are strategy classes that implement `com.hazelcast.merge.MergePolicy`, we can create our own but there are a number of provided instances available to us out of the box.

- `hz.NO_MERGE`, which is a non-operation policy, no entries will be merged.

- `hz.ADD_NEW_ENTRY`, where the entry will be added if it did not already exist within the cluster.

- `hz.HIGHER_HITS`, which merges depending on the amount of activity on a particular entry on either side of the split. Whichever version of the entry had been interacted with the most will win.

- `hz.LATEST_UPDATE`, probably the most useful, whichever version the entry had most recently been created or updated will be the copy to retain.

The configuration is applied as part of the standard collection configuration; unless we specify our own, the default is currently `hz.ADD_NEW_ENTRY`.

```
<hazelcast>
  <map name="default">
    <merge-policy>hz.LATEST_UPDATE</merge-policy>
  </map>
</hazelcast>
```

If we do create our own merge policy class we will need to register it before we are able to use it. We wire up our class name to a merge policy name, to which we refer to in our collection configuration.

```
<hazelcast>
  <map name="default">
    <merge-policy>OUR_MERGE_POLICY</merge-policy>
  </map>

  <merge-policies>
    <map-merge-policy name="OUR_MERGE_POLICY">
      <class-name>
        com.packtpub.hazelcast.OurMergePolicy
      </class-name>
    </map-merge-policy>
  </merge-policies>
</hazelcast>
```

Summary

So we now know a little more of how Hazelcast apportions data into partitions, how these partitions are automatically assigned to a node or a partition group and how we might configure these to our needs. We have also investigated how it deals with issues, be it failure of an individual node or group of nodes within a defined silo, and how we recover it to restore resilience; or an underlying network fabric issue that creates a network split brain, and how we are able to cleanly bring multiple sides of the split back together and return to normal service.

Now that we have seen how things work behind the scenes to manage and distribute our data, we might need our application to know about some of these goings-on. In the next chapter we shall look at how our application can register its interest to be notified as things happen to support the cluster.

5
Listening Out

In a broad, distributed cluster of data storage, it is very useful to be able to know what is happening with our data, either to trigger an application-level response to an event, or to purely give us some visibility to the internal goings-on. In this chapter, we will learn about:

- Creating and using collection listeners
- Instance, lifecycle, and cluster membership listeners
- Partition migration listener

Listening to the goings-on

One great feature of Hazelcast is its ability to notify us of the goings-on of our persisted data and the cluster as a whole. To allow us to register an interest in events, the listener concept is borrowed from Java. In that way, there are a number of listener interfaces that we can implement to receive, process, and handle different types of events; one of which we have previously encountered.

- Collection listeners
    - `EntryListener` for map-based (`IMap` and `MultiMap`) events
    - `ItemListener` for flat collection-based (`IList`, `ISet`, and `IQueue`) events
    - `MessageListener` for receiving topic events, but as we've seen before, it is used as part of the standard operation of topics

- Cluster listeners
    - `InstanceListener` for collection, creation, and destruction events
    - `MembershipListener` for cluster membership events
    - `LifecycleListener` for local node state events
    - `MigrationListener` for partition migration state events

The sound of our own data

Being notified as our data changes can be rather useful, so we can make an application-level decision on whether that change is important or not. The first interface we are going to look at is `EntryListener`. This class will notify us when changes are made to the entries stored in a map collection. If we take a look at the interface, we can see four event types that we will be notified about.

```
public interface EntryListener<K, V> extends EventListener {
  void entryAdded(EntryEvent<K, V> event);
  void entryRemoved(EntryEvent<K, V> event);
  void entryUpdated(EntryEvent<K, V> event);
  void entryEvicted(EntryEvent<K, V> event);
}
```

Hopefully, the first three are pretty self-explanatory; however, the last is a little less clear and in fact, one of the most useful. The `entryEvicted` method is invoked when an entry is removed from a map non-programmatically (that is, Hazelcast has done it all by itself). This instance will occur in one of two scenarios:

- An entry's TTL has been reached and the entry has been expired
- The map size according to the configured policy has been reached, and the appropriate eviction policy has been kicked in to clear out space in the map

The first scenario allows us a capability very rarely found in data sources, to have our application be told when a time bound record has expired, and the ability to trigger some behavior based on it. For example, we could use it to automatically trigger a teardown operation, should an entry not be correctly maintained by a user's interactions. This would allow us to generate an event based on the absence of activity, which is rather useful!

Let's create an example `MapEntryListener` to illustrate the various events firing off.

```
public class MapEntryListener
  implements EntryListener<String, String> {

  @Override
  public void entryAdded(EntryEvent<String, String> event) {
    System.err.println("Added: " + event);
  }

  @Override
  public void entryRemoved(EntryEvent<String, String> event) {
    System.err.println("Removed: " + event);
  }
```

```
@Override
public void entryUpdated(EntryEvent<String, String> event) {
  System.err.println("Updated: " + event);
}

@Override
public void entryEvicted(EntryEvent<String, String> event) {
  System.err.println("Evicted: " + event);
}
}
```

We can use it in conjunction with MapEntryListeningExample to drive some behavior.

```
public class MapEntryListeningExample {
  public static void main(String[] args) {
    HazelcastInstance hz = Hazelcast.newHazelcastInstance();

    IMap<String, String> capitals = hz.getMap("capitals");
    capitals.addEntryListener(new MapEntryListener(), true);

    capitals.put("GB", "Winchester");
    capitals.put("GB", "London");
    capitals.put("DE", "Berlin", 10, TimeUnit.SECONDS);
    capitals.remove("GB");
  }
}
```

We shall see the various events firing off as expected, with a short 10-second wait for the Berlin entry to expire, which will trigger the eviction event.

```
Added: EntryEvent {c:capitals} key=GB, oldValue=null, value=Winchester,
event=ADDED, by Member [127.0.0.1]:5701 this


Updated: EntryEvent {c:capitals} key=GB, oldValue=Winchester,
value=London, event=UPDATED, by Member [127.0.0.1]:5701 this


Added: EntryEvent {c:capitals} key=DE, oldValue=null, value=Berlin,
event=ADDED, by Member [127.0.0.1]:5701 this


Removed: EntryEvent {c:capitals} key=GB, oldValue=null, value=London,
event=REMOVED, by Member [127.0.0.1]:5701 this
```

```
Evicted: EntryEvent {c:capitals} key=DE, oldValue=null, value=Berlin,
event=EVICTED, by Member [127.0.0.1]:5701 this
```

We can obviously implement the interface as extensively as needed to service our application, potentially creating no-op stubs should we wish not to handle a particular type of event.

One issue with the previous example is that we have retrospectively reconfigured the map to feature the listener after it is already in service. To avoid this race condition, we should wire up the listen in advance of our node-entering service. We can do this by registering the listener within the map configuration.

```
<hazelcast>
  <map name="default">
    <entry-listeners>
      <entry-listener include-value="true">
        com.packtpub.hazelcast.listeners.MapEntryListener
      </entry-listener>
    </entry-listeners>
  </map>
</hazelcast>
```

But in both the methods of configuration, we have provided a Boolean flag when registering the listener to the map. This include-value flag allows us to configure it when the listener is invoked, whether or not we are interested in just the key of the event entry, or the all the data including the entries value. The default behavior (true) is to include the value, but suppose our use case does not require it, there is a performance benefit of not having to provide it to the listener.

Keyless collections

While very similar to map collections, the keyless collections (set, list, and queue) feature their own interface to define the available events, in this case ItemListener. It is not as extensive as its map counterpart, featuring just itemAdded and itemRemoved events, and can be used in the same way but with a lesser degree of visibility.

Programmatic configuration ahead of time

So far the extra configurations we have applied have either been by customizing the `hazelcast.xml` file, or retrospectively modifying a collection in the code. But what if we want to programmatically configure Hazelcast, without the race condition we discovered earlier? Fortunately, there is such a way. By creating an instance of the `Config` class, we can configure the appropriate behavior on it using a similar hierarchy to the XML configuration, but in code. Before passing this configuration object over to the instance creation method, the previous example could be reconfigured to do so.

```
public static void main(String[] args) {
  Config conf = new Config();
  conf.addListenerConfig(new ListenerConfig(new MapEntryListener()));

  HazelcastInstance hz = Hazelcast.newHazelcastInstance(conf);
```

Events unfolding in the wider world

Now that we can determine what is going on with our data within the cluster, we might wish to have a degree of visibility of the state of the cluster itself. We could use this to trigger application-level responses to cluster instability, or provide mechanisms to enable graceful scaling. We are provided with a number of interfaces for different types of cluster activity. All of these listeners can be configured retrospectively as we have seen in our previous examples; however, in production, it would be better to configure them in advance for the same race condition reasons as the collection listeners. We can either do this using the `hazelcast.xml` configuration or by using the `Config` class.

```
<hazelcast>
  <listeners>
    <listener>com.packtpub.hazelcast.MyClusterListener</listener>
  </listeners>
</hazelcast>
```

The first of these, `InstanceListener`, simply notifies all the nodes in the cluster as to new collection instances being created or having been destroyed. Again, let's create a new example listener `ClusterInstanceListener` to receive events.

```
public class ClusterInstanceListener implements InstanceListener {

  @Override
  public void instanceCreated(InstanceEvent event) {
```

```
    System.err.println("Created: " + event);
  }

  @Override
  public void instanceDestroyed(InstanceEvent event) {
    System.err.println("Destroyed: " + event);
  }
}
```

As these listeners are for cluster-wide events, our example usage of this listener is rather simple, mainly creating an instance with the appropriate listener registered.

```
public class ClusterListeningExample {
  public static void main(String[] args) {
    Config config = new Config();
    config.addListenerConfig(
      new ListenerConfig(new ClusterInstanceListener()));

    HazelcastInstance hz = Hazelcast.newHazelcastInstance(config);
  }
}
```

In using our `TestApp` console, we can create and destroy some collections.

```
hazelcast[default] > ns test
namespace: test


hazelcast[test] > m.put foo bar
null


hazelcast[test] > m.destroy
Destroyed!
```

This will produce the following logging on all our nodes that feature the listener:

```
Created: com.hazelcast.core.InstanceEvent[source=Map [test] ]
Destroyed: com.hazelcast.core.InstanceEvent[source=Map [test] ]
```

The next type of cluster listener is `MembershipListener`, which notifies all nodes as to the joining or leaving of a node from the cluster. Let's create another example class, this time `ClusterMembershipListener`.

```
public class ClusterMembershipListener
    implements MembershipListener {
```

```
@Override
public void memberAdded(MembershipEvent membershipEvent) {
  System.err.println("Added: " + membershipEvent);
}

@Override
public void memberRemoved(MembershipEvent membershipEvent) {
  System.err.println("Removed: " + membershipEvent);
}
}
```

And add it to our previous example application.

```
conf.addListenerConfig(
  new ListenerConfig(new ClusterMembershipListener()));
```

Lastly, we have `LifecycleListener`, which is local to an individual node, and allows our application built on top of Hazelcast to understand its particular node state by being notified as it changes while starting, pausing, resuming, or even shutting down.

```
public class NodeLifecycleListener implements LifecycleListener {

  @Override
  public void stateChanged(LifecycleEvent event) {
    System.err.println(event);
  }
}
```

Moving data around the place

The final listener is very useful as it lets our application know when Hazelcast is rebalancing the data within the cluster. This allows us the opportunity to prevent or even block the shutdown of a node as we might be in a period of increased data resilience risk. The interface used for this case is `MigrationListener` and will notify our application as partitions are migrated from one node to another and when they have completed.

```
public class ClusterMigrationListener implements MigrationListener {

  @Override
  public void migrationStarted(MigrationEvent migrationEvent) {
    System.err.println("Started: " + migrationEvent);
  }
```

```
@Override
public void migrationCompleted(MigrationEvent migrationEvent) {
  System.err.println("Completed: " + migrationEvent);
}

@Override
public void migrationFailed(MigrationEvent migrationEvent) {
  System.err.println("Failed: " + migrationEvent);
}
}
```

In registering this cluster listener in our example application and creating and destroying various nodes, we should see a deluge of events showing the migrations occurring. The more astute among you may have previously spotted a repartitioning task logging when spinning up multiple nodes.

```
INFO: [127.0.0.1]:5701 [dev] Re-partitioning cluster data... Immediate-
Tasks: 0, Scheduled-Tasks: 271
```

This indicated that 271 tasks (one migration task for each partition) have been scheduled to rebalance the cluster. Our new listener will now give us significantly more visibility on these events as they occur and hopefully they will be completed successfully.

```
Started: MigrationEvent{partitionId=98, oldOwner=Member [127.0.0.1]:5701,
newOwner=Member [127.0.0.1]:5702 this}


Started: MigrationEvent{partitionId=99, oldOwner=Member [127.0.0.1]:5701,
newOwner=Member [127.0.0.1]:5702 this}


Completed: MigrationEvent{partitionId=98, oldOwner=Member
[127.0.0.1]:5701, newOwner=Member [127.0.0.1]:5702 this}


Completed: MigrationEvent{partitionId=99, oldOwner=Member
[127.0.0.1]:5701, newOwner=Member [127.0.0.1]:5702 this}
```

However, all this logging information is entirely overwhelming and not that useful to us, so let's expand on our listener to try and provide our application with the ability to detect if our cluster is currently migrating data partitions or has recently done so.

Let's create a new static class `MigrationStatus` to hold cluster migration information and allow us to interrogate it as the current status.

```java
public abstract class MigrationStatus {
  private static final Map<Integer, Boolean> MIGRATION_STATE =
    new ConcurrentHashMap<Integer, Boolean>();

  private static final AtomicLong LAST_MIGRATION_TIME =
    new AtomicLong(System.currentTimeMillis());

  public static void migrationEvent(int partitionId, boolean state) {
    MIGRATION_STATE.put(partitionId, state);
    if (!state) {
      LAST_MIGRATION_TIME.set(System.currentTimeMillis());
    }
  }

  public static boolean isMigrating() {
    Collection<Boolean> migrationStates = MIGRATION_STATE.values();
    Long lastMigrationTime = LAST_MIGRATION_TIME.get();

    // did we recently (< 10 seconds ago) complete a migration
    if (System.currentTimeMillis() < lastMigrationTime + 10000) {
      return true;
    }

    // are any partitions currently migrating
    for (Boolean partition : migrationStates) {
      if (partition) {
        return true;
      }
    }

    // otherwise we're not migrating
    return false;
  }
}
```

Then we update our listener to pass through the appropriate calls in response to the events coming into it.

```java
@Override
  public void migrationStarted(MigrationEvent migrationEvent) {
    MigrationStatus.migrationEvent(
      migrationEvent.getPartitionId(), true);
```

```
    }

    @Override
    public void migrationCompleted(MigrationEvent migrationEvent) {
      MigrationStatus.migrationEvent(
        migrationEvent.getPartitionId(), false);
    }

    @Override
    public void migrationFailed(MigrationEvent migrationEvent) {
      System.err.println("Failed: " + migrationEvent);
      MigrationStatus.migrationEvent(
        migrationEvent.getPartitionId(), false);
    }
```

Finally, let's add a loop to our example application to print out the migration state over time.

```
    public static void main(String[] args) throws Exception {
        Config conf = new Config();
        conf.addListenerConfig(
          new ListenerConfig(new ClusterMembershipListener()));
        conf.addListenerConfig(
          new ListenerConfig(new MigrationStatusListener()));

        HazelcastInstance hz = Hazelcast.newHazelcastInstance(conf);

        while(true) {
          System.err.println(
            "Is Migrating?: " + MigrationStatus.isMigrating());
          Thread.sleep(5000);
        }
    }
```

In starting and stopping various nodes, we should see each node detect the presence of rebalance occurring, but it passes by quite quickly. It is in these small critical periods of time when data is being moved around that resilience is most at risk, albeit depending on the configured numbers of backup, the risk could potentially be quite small.

```
Added: MembershipEvent {Member [127.0.0.1]:5703} added

Is Migrating?: true

Is Migrating?: true

Is Migrating?: false
```

Summary

Unlike some of its peers, Hazelcast allows us to witness first hand a lot of internal state information. By registering listeners to be notified as events occur, we can further enhance our application not only in terms of functionality but also in resilience. By allowing our application to know when and what events are unfolding underneath it, we can add defensiveness to it—embracing the dynamic and destroyable nature of modern agile approaches to applications and infrastructure.

In the next chapter, we will move a little away from just data, and look at the distributed execution and task processing capabilities on offer.

6
Spreading the Load

In addition to the distributed data storage, Hazelcast also provides us with an ability to share out computational power, in the form of a distributed executor. In this chapter, we shall:

- Learn about the distributed executor service
- Using futures for response retrieval
- Single node and multi-node tasks
- Forcing the location of execution
- Aligning data with compute

All power to the compute

So far, we have been focusing on data storage for a lot of cases that would take up most of the story for scaling up our application. However, there are other types of applications that require a lot of computational and data processing power. To help cater for this use case, Hazelcast provides a distributed executor service. For us relatively experienced Java developers, we are hopefully already familiar with the introduction of ExecutorService with Java v1.5. Extending this concept further, the distributed execution capabilities allow us to run the Runnable and Callable tasks on the cluster. However, as we are distributing the task, we must ensure that it is also Serializable.

We can think of Hazelcast as providing the scheduling and task management capabilities on top of a number of executors, holding a number of worker threads each.

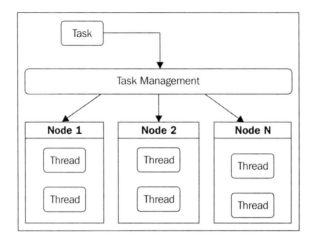

Like the data storage capabilities offered, should we need to add further capacity to the cluster, we can start more nodes. This will immediately register their presence to the cluster and be available to provide extra computational power. To see this working, let's create an example `TimeCallable` task to execute.

```
public class TimeCallable implements Callable<String>, Serializable {

  @Override
  public String call() throws Exception {
    return new Date().toString();
  }
}
```

Also, create an example application to submit the task for execution as well as the computation needed to process the running of the task. To get the return value from the `Callable` task, we will need to use a `Future` reference to simplify our example. For the moment, we will use the blocking `get()` operation that will await a response before continuing.

```
public class ExecutionExample {
  public static void main(String[] args) throws Exception {
    Config conf = new Config();
    HazelcastInstance hz = Hazelcast.newHazelcastInstance(conf);

    ExecutorService exec = hz.getExecutorService("exec");
```

```
      while(true) {
        Future<String> timeFuture = exec.submit(new TimeCallable());
        String theTime = timeFuture.get();

        System.err.println(theTime);

        Thread.sleep(1000);
      }
    }
  }
```

We can create a number of nodes that will increase the processing capacity of the cluster; however, if we did so with our current example, it wouldn't be obvious from our example where the task was actually running. In fact, some tasks might actually need to know where they are running; luckily, we can update our `Callable` task with where it is running through the use of the `HazelcastInstanceAware` interface. This will inform the task with a reference to the appropriate instance prior to the task execution.

```
public class TimeInstanceAwareCallable
    implements Callable<String>, HazelcastInstanceAware, Serializable {

    private HazelcastInstance hz;

    @Override
    public void setHazelcastInstance(HazelcastInstance hz) {
      this.hz = hz;
    }

    @Override
    public String call() throws Exception {
      return hz.getCluster().getLocalMember().toString() +
      " - " + new Date().toString();
    }
}
```

In running our application and having updated it to use our instance aware task, we should now see that the execution is being shared across multiple nodes.

```
Member [127.0.0.1]:5701 this - Tue Jan 01 00:00:01 UTC 2013
Member [127.0.0.1]:5702 this - Tue Jan 01 00:00:02 UTC 2013
```

Giving up when tasks take too long

In using the blocking get() function, we might end up waiting for a very long time should the computation be extensive or complex. Should we have an SLA that we need to meet and there is no point continuing the processing if we breach it, we can specific this timeout on the retrieval call. This has the added benefit of automatically canceling the processing task should the timeout be reached, freeing up the compute resource for other tasks.

Running once, running everywhere

So far we've seen how we can gain access to a distributed executor service and submit our own tasks to it for execution; however, we might need a little more control as to where a task runs. Should we want to pin a particular task to a specific node, we can use the wrapper class DistributedTask to provide some signaling logic to the task manager so that it can detect and control which node the task is delegated to. You can find the details of the members in the cluster from the Cluster class, which is accessible from the HazelcastInstance class.

```
Config conf = new Config();
HazelcastInstance hz = Hazelcast.newHazelcastInstance(conf);

Member thisMember = hz.getCluster().getLocalMember();
Set<Member> clusterMembers = hz.getCluster().getMembers();
ExecutorService exec = hz.getExecutorService("exec");

Callable<String> timeTask = new TimeInstanceAwareCallable();

Member member = <target member>;
FutureTask<String> specificTask =
  new DistributedTask<String>(timeTask, member);

exec.execute(specificTask);
String timeFromSpecificMember =
  specificTask.get(10, TimeUnit.SECONDS);
```

Should we want to run the task on multiple nodes concurrently, we could manually submit the task to multiple specific member nodes. However, it would be complicated to retrieve the results of each execution, especially if the ordering of the responses is not sequential. To help address this issue, there is another wrapper class we can use, MultiTask, which is similar to our previous example. However, it handles the capture and aggregation of various responses for us.

```
public class MultiExecutionExample {
  public static void main(String[] args) throws Exception {
    Config conf = new Config();
```

```
HazelcastInstance hz = Hazelcast.newHazelcastInstance(conf);

ExecutorService exec = hz.getExecutorService("exec");

Callable<String> timeCallable = new TimeInstanceAwareCallable();

while(true) {
  Set<Member> clusterMembers = hz.getCluster().getMembers();

  MultiTask<String> timeTask =
    new MultiTask<String>(timeCallable, clusterMembers);

  exec.execute(timeTask);
  Collection<String> manyTimes = timeTask.get();

  for (String theTime : manyTimes) {
    System.err.println("The time is: " + theTime);
  }

  Thread.sleep(1000);
  }
 }
}
```

Quite usefully, Hazelcast provides us with a few tasks that we can use to gather some operation stats on the members in the cluster, the collections in use, the amount of data stored, and the number of requests we are making to them. These tasks can be found in the main Hazelcast JAR within the com.hazelcast.monitor package. Let's have a look at one of these to get high-level partition assignment information from the cluster.

```
public class MemberInfoStatsExample {
  public static void main(String[] args) throws Exception {
    Config conf = new Config();
    HazelcastInstance hz = Hazelcast.newHazelcastInstance(conf);

    ExecutorService exec = hz.getExecutorService();
    MultiTask<MemberInfo> mapStatsTask =
      new MultiTask<MemberInfo>(
        new DistributedMemberInfoCallable(),
        hz.getCluster().getMembers());

    exec.execute(mapStatsTask);

    for(MemberInfo memberInfo : mapStatsTask.get()) {
```

```
        System.err.println("partitions: " +
          memberInfo.getPartitions().size());
      }
    }
  }
```

In running the application once, we'll see all the partitions belonging to one node before any new instances will see this increasingly more distributed.

// 1 node

partitions: 271

// 2 nodes

partitions: 136

partitions: 135

// 3 nodes

partitions: 91

partitions: 90

partitions: 90

Placing tasks next to the data

Our capability to run a task in a specific target location becomes much more useful when it comes to data affinity. This means that if we are going to be interacting with the distributed data held within the cluster, it would be optimal to co-locate the task execution close to where the required data is actually held. This will reduce the latency of a task and the networking cost of having to retrieve the dependency data from other nodes across the cluster before processing can actually occur. By making our task PartitionAware, we can return a key with which our task is going to interact. From this it is established which partition the key belongs to, and hence the member node that holds that data. Then the task will be automatically submitted to execute on that specific node to minimize the network latency for the task to obtain or manipulate the data.

We might also need to interact with multiple related entries, which might belong to different partitions, hence be owned by other members. If the relationship between the two entries is strictly coupled, we could consider overriding the standard partitioning process by providing a specific value to pass on to the partitioning hash function. This will have the effect of allowing a set of data to be guaranteed to belong to a shared partition, even if we don't know which one or where. To do this, we will need to make our persisted class `PartitionAware`. Let's extend our previous city model POJO from the previous chapter. I would suggest that cities within the same country are likely to be coupled (in the data sense at least).

```
public class City implements PartitionAware, Serializable {

<snip>

  @Override
  public Object getPartitionKey() {
    return country;
  }
}
```

From this, we could build a number of processing tasks that could search, process, and return results; say, find us the average population size for our cities for a particular country. Implement the same `PartitionAware` interface in the same way as our persisted class so that our task and supporting data will co-locate.

```
public class AverageCityPopulationCallable
    implements Callable<Integer>, HazelcastInstanceAware,
      PartitionAware, Serializable {

  private String country;
  private HazelcastInstance hz;

  public AverageCityPopulationCallable(String country) {
    this.country = country;
  }

  @Override
  public void setHazelcastInstance(HazelcastInstance hz) {
    this.hz = hz;
  }

  @Override
  public Object getPartitionKey() {
    return country;
  }
```

```
@Override
public Integer call() throws Exception {
  System.err.println("Running task on: " +
    hz.getCluster().getLocalMember().toString());

  IMap<String, City> cities = hz.getMap("cities");
  Predicate countryCityPredicate =
    Predicates.equal(Predicates.get("country"), country);
  Collection<City> countryCities =
    cities.values(countryCityPredicate);

  int totalPopulation = 0;
  for (City countryCity : countryCities) {
    totalPopulation += countryCity.getPopulation();
  }

  return totalPopulation / countryCities.size();
  }
}
```

In using this task against a small dataset, we can see the operation in action.

```
public class AverageCityPopulationCallableExample {
  public static void main(String[] args) throws Exception {
    Config conf = new Config();
    MapConfig citiesConf = conf.getMapConfig("cities");
    citiesConf.addMapIndexConfig(
      new MapIndexConfig("country", false));

    HazelcastInstance hz = Hazelcast.newHazelcastInstance(conf);

    IMap<String, City> cities = hz.getMap("cities");

    if (cities.isEmpty()) {
      cities.put("London-GB",
        new City("London", "GB", 8174100));
      cities.put("Southampton-GB",
        new City("Southampton", "GB", 304400));
      cities.put("Plymouth-GB",
        new City("Plymouth", "GB", 258700));
      cities.put("York-GB",
        new City("York", "GB", 197800));

      cities.put("Paris-FR",
        new City("Paris", "FR", 2268265));
    }
```

```
ExecutorService exec = hz.getExecutorService();

Future<Integer> avgTask = exec.submit(
  new AverageCityPopulationCallable("GB"));

Integer avgPop = avgTask.get();
System.err.println("Average GB city population: " + avgPop);
    }
}
```

Self-updating results

This type of execution is great if we need real time results for each operation requiring this value; however, if this was a more computationally expensive operation, we will still need fast access to this data but perhaps on more of a best effort basis. Rather than returning sequentially, we could create a `Runnable` task to run, periodically storing the result into another collection for consumption. This is akin to pre-aggregation as you would just retrieve the value from the output collection knowing that the value must have been generated in the background, and depending on the data, the frequency of execution might be slightly out of date. However, we can configure how stale it could be based on our application's own needs.

```
public class AverageCityPopulationRunnable
    implements Runnable, HazelcastInstanceAware, Serializable {

<snip>

  @Override
  public void run() {

    int avgPopulation = totalPopulation / countryCities.size();
    IMap<String, Integer> avgCityPop = hz.getMap("cityAvgPop");
    avgCityPop.put(country, avgPopulation);
  }
}
```

Summary

As we can see, this is a technology that deals with many aspects of distribution, be it data persistence or even computation. By leveraging these capabilities into our architecture, we are providing ourselves with a very simple scaling mechanism— just add more nodes. We are scaling up multiple aspects of our application simultaneously; in this way, we should hopefully not introduce any scaling imbalances that might have been present if we had just scaled one aspect independently.

In the next chapter, we will examine the different architectural setups that Hazelcast can operate in, the situations that suit the various options, and how to use them.

7
Typical Deployments

So far we have been looking at Hazelcast in one particular type of deployment, however, there are a number of configurations we could use depending on our particular architecture and application needs. Each deployment strategy tends to be best suited to certain types of configuration or application deployment; so in this chapter we will look at:

- The issues of co-locating data too close to the application
- Thin client connectivity, where it's best used and the issues that come with it
- Lite member node (nee super client) as a middle ground option
- Overview of the architectural choices

All heap and nowhere to go

One thing we may have noticed with all the examples we have been working on so far is that as we are running Hazelcast in an embedded mode, each of the JVM instances will provide both the application's functionality and also house the data storage. Hence the persisted cluster data is held within the heap of the various nodes, but this does mean that we will need to control the provisioned heap sizes more accurately as it is now more than just a non-functional advantage to have more; size matters.

However, depending on the type of application we are developing, it may not be convenient or suitable to directly use the application's heap on the running instance for storing in the data. A pertinent example of this situation would be a web application, especially one that runs in a potentially shared web application container (for example, Apache Tomcat).

This would be rather unsuitable for storing extensive amounts of data within the heap as our application's storage requirements drastically increase, we will either need to provision more web application containers, or potentially put ours and other applications running with that container cluster at risk from excessive garbage collection, or worse still running out of heap altogether.

Stepping back from the cluster

To avoid this situation we can separate our application away from the data cluster through the use of a thin client driver that looks and appears very similar to a direct Hazelcast instance; however, in this case, the operations performed are delegated out to a wider cluster of real instances. This has the benefit of separating our application away from the scaling of the Hazelcast cluster, allowing us to scale up our own application without having to scale everything together, maximizing the utilization efficiency of the resources we are running on. However, we can still scale up our data cluster by adding more nodes which will lead to a bottleneck, either for memory storage requirements or performance and compute necessities.

If we create a "server side" vanilla instance to provide us with a cluster of nodes we can connect out to from a client.

```
public class VanillaInstanceExample {
  public static void main(String[] args) {
    Config conf = new Config();
    HazelcastInstance hz = Hazelcast.newHazelcastInstance(conf);
  }
}
```

If we run this a few times to establish a cluster of a number of instances:

```
Members [3] {
    Member [127.0.0.1]:5701
    Member [127.0.0.1]:5702
    Member [127.0.0.1]:5703 this
}
```

Now we need to bring in a new dependency, with our original downloaded archive is the `hazelcast-client-2.6.jar`, and we can use this to create `ClientExample` to connect to the cluster and perform operations against the data that is held there. As the client is delegating the operations out to the wider cluster, the data persisted will out-live the client.

```
public class ClientExample {
  public static void main(String[] args) {
    ClientConfig conf = new ClientConfig();
    conf.addAddress("127.0.0.1:5701");

    HazelcastClient hzc =
      HazelcastClient.newHazelcastClient(conf);

    IMap<String, String> capitals = hzc.getMap("capitals");
```

```
if (capitals.isEmpty()) {
  System.err.println("Empty capitals map, adding entries");

  capitals.put("GB", "London");
  capitals.put("FR", "Paris");
  capitals.put("US", "Washington DC");
  capitals.put("AU", "Canberra");
}

System.err.println(
  "Known capital cities: " + capitals.size());

System.err.println(
  "Capital city of GB: " + capitals.get("GB"));

hzc.shutdown();
  }
}
```

In running our client multiple times we can see that the first run will initialize the capitals map with our starting set of data, before shutting down the client which will allow the JVM instance to complete and exit cleanly. However, when we run the client again, the data has been successfully persisted by the still running cluster so that we won't repopulate it a second time. Our client is currently connecting through to one of the clients specifically, however it learns about the existence of the other nodes once it is running. So should our supporting member node die, the client will simply connect over to another one of the other nodes and continue on as normal. The only critical phase is the initial connection, that unlike the member nodes we don't have an auto-discovery mechanism in place; so that needs to be configured explicitly. If the node we have listed is down at the time of our client starting up, we will fail to connect to the cluster irrespective of the state of other nodes or the cluster as a whole. We can address this by listing a number of seed nodes within our client's configuration, as long as one of these nodes is available we can connect to the cluster and go from there.

```
ClientConfig conf = new ClientConfig();
conf.addAddress("127.0.0.1:5701");
conf.addAddress("127.0.0.1:5702", "127.0.0.1:5703");
```

By default, the ordering of the nodes we attempt to connect to is consistent depending on the configuration, should the first nodes we try to connect to be down or having networking issues, we might have to wait until the configured connection time-out to be reached before moving on to the next to try block. To prevent a consistent issue proving to be an ongoing issue for clients starting up, we can set the client to randomly order the target nodes list from its configuration. In this way we would get a faster connection time, at least for a proportion of the time, this may be preferable to a possible consistent issue.

```
conf.setShuffle(true);
```

Serialization and classes

One issue we do introduce when using the thin client driver( )is that while our cluster can hold, persist, and serve classes it doesn't have to and might not actually hold the **POJO** class itself; rather a serialization of the object. This means that as long as each of our clients holds the appropriate class in its classpath we can successfully serialize (for persistence) and de-serialize (for retrieval), but our cluster nodes can't. You can most notably see this if we try to retrieve entries via the `TestApp` console for custom objects, this will produce `ClassNotFoundException`.

The process used to serialize objects to the cluster starts by checking whether the object is a well-known primitive-like class (`String`, `Long`, `Integer`, `byte[]`, `ByteBuffer`, `Date`); if so, these are serialized directly. If not, Hazelcast next checks to see if the object implements `com.hazelcast.nio.DataSerializable` and if so uses the appropriate methods provided to marshal the object. Otherwise it falls back to standard Java serialization.

However in the case of using the distributed executor, as the execution will actually be performed on the cluster nodes themselves, those classes must be present on the classpath of each cluster node.

Lite cluster members

One issue with the client method of connecting to the cluster is that most operations will require multiple hops in order to perform an action. This is as we only maintain a connection to a single node of the cluster and run all our operations through it. With the exception of operations performed on partitions owned by that node, all other activities must be handed off to the node responsible out in the wider cluster, with the single node acting as a proxy for the client.

This will add latency to the requests made to the cluster. Should that latency be too high, there is an alternative method of connecting to the cluster known as a lite member (originally known as a super client). This is effectively a non-participant member of the cluster, in that it maintains connections to all the other nodes in the cluster and will directly talk to partition owners, but does not provide any storage or computation to the cluster. This avoids the double hop required by the standard client, but adds the additional complexity and overhead of participating in the cluster. For most uses cases using the standard client is preferable as it is much simpler to configure and use, and can work over higher latency connections; however, should you need higher levels of performance and throughput, you could consider using a lite member.

Lite members are set up as you would set up a standard node, hence the additional complexity is involved; however with one small addition in the configuration that flags the node as being non-participant.

```
Config conf = new Config();
conf.setLiteMember(true);
```

When a lite member is present in the cluster the other members will be aware of its presence and the fact that it is such a type of node. You will see the appropriate logging in the startup and cluster state logging on the various cluster nodes.

```
Members [3] {
    Member [127.0.0.1]:5701 this
    Member [127.0.0.1]:5702
    Member [127.0.0.1]:5703 lite
}
```

Architectural overview

As we have seen there are a number of different types of deployment we could use, which one you choose really depends on our application's make up. Each has a number of trade-offs but most deployments tend to use one of the first two, with the client and server cluster approach the usual favorite unless we have a mostly compute focused application where the former is a simpler set up.

So let's have a look at the various architectural setups we could employ and what situations they are best suited to.

Peer-to-peer cluster

This is the standard example we have been mostly using until now, each node houses both our application itself, and data persistence and processing. It is most useful when we have an application that is primarily focused towards asynchronous or high performance computing, and will be executing lots of tasks on the cluster. The greatest drawback is the inability to scale our application and data capacity separately.

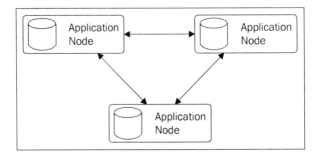

Clients and server cluster

This is a more appropriate setup for the situation where we are mostly storing data in our cluster rather than running tasks. A cluster of *server* nodes is independently created, scaled, and managed. It is then interacted to via a thin client driver from our application. While this provides good separation between our application and the Hazelcast cluster, it does require more awareness of the classpaths of both our application and the cluster nodes.

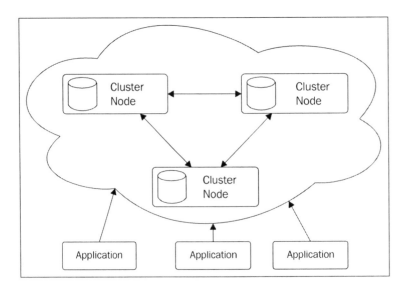

Hybrid cluster

A middle ground between the two previous strategies, the creation and management of a primary cluster of nodes with a shadow set, holds the application's capabilities but none of the data or computation responsibilities. The only real use case for this strategy is where the client option doesn't provide the required latency, and performance demands from our application due to having to leap frog through other nodes in the cluster to get at our data.

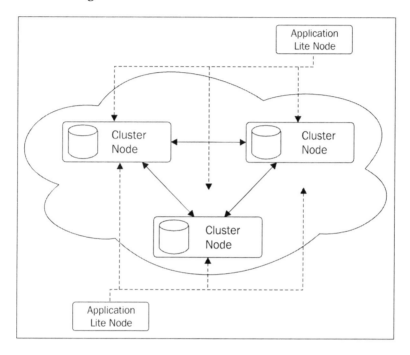

Summary

We have seen that we have a number of strategies at our deposal for deploying Hazelcast within our architecture. Be it, treating it like a clustered standalone product akin to a traditional data source but with more resilience and scalability. For more complex applications we can directly absorb the capabilities directly into our application, but that does come with some strings attached. But whichever approach we choose for our particular use case, we have easy access to scaling and control at our finger tips.

In the next chapter we will look beyond just Hazelcast and the alternative methods of getting access to our held data in the cluster.

From the Outside Looking In

In addition to the standard native client access to the cluster, Hazelcast also provides a few generic interfaces itself so that our application be powered by a technology stack that isn't necessarily Java-based, and we can still take advantage of some its capabilities:

- Memcache compatible access to the default map
- RESTful access to map and queue collections

What about the rest of us?

One limitation of Hazelcast is that due to being a Java-based technology it is mostly focused on supporting applications build around that stack. While we do have a degree of flexibility, in that, other JVM byte-code based languages (such as Groovy or Scala) can utilize the standard Java client driver, but that still does leave a rather large hole for other technology choices. Luckily and very thoughtfully, the cluster nodes do offer limited access to some of our data storage collections in a more compatible way using two popular standards.

Memcache

If we were building a script-based application (say in Python or PHP), and required a data caching service, probably one of the first systems we would consider would be memcache. Both incredibly fast and remarkably simple, but it is this simplicity that does come with some drawbacks. Currently to provide resilience or replication, we have to either handle it on the client side or overlay another system on top of the default memcache to provide transparent scaling or data sharing. But either way, we are exposing some consistency risks, especially in the case of node failure or fallover.

However, one of its greatest strengths is the extent of its client libraries, with no fewer than 10 different technology stacks catered for. Drawing upon these benefits

Hazelcast has sought to provide a compatible alternative, in exposing a memcache API service from each of the Hazelcast cluster nodes. As each of the nodes exposes access to the whole cluster, we can talk to any node about any key held wherever it may be. However, as the memcache API only offers access to a single giant map, we initially interact to the **default** map collection as provided by Hazelcast. But if we wish to interact with another map we can do so by prefixing the key with the map name and a colon (for example, `countries:GB`).

We must also limit all the serialization to the client side and to the key and value offering provided by the memcache API. This does mean we will have to be careful not to use this map by non-memcache clients, as we might create data that cannot be read by these clients.

We can create a few examples using an appropriate client for a couple of popular technology choices.

In Python, using the python-memcached client:

```python
#!/usr/bin/env python
import memcache

mc = memcache.Client(["127.0.0.1:5701"], debug=0)

city = {
  "name": "London",
  "country": "GB",
  "population": 8174100
}

mc.set("London-GB", city)

london = mc.get("London-GB")

print london
```

And in PHP, we can use the **PECL Memcache extension**:

```php
<?php

$mc = new Memcache();
$mc->connect("127.0.0.1", 5701)
  or die("Could not connect to Hazelcast");

$city = Array();
```

```php
$city["name"] = "London";
$city["country"] = "GB";
$city["population"] = 8174100;


$mc->set("London-GB", $city)
  or die("Failed to save city");


$london = $mc->get("London-GB");


echo var_export($london, true) ."\n";


?>
```

which will save and persist the value to the Hazelcast cluster and retrieve as required.

```
$ pyton memcache_example.py
{'country': 'GB', 'name': 'London', 'population': 8174100}

$ php -f memcache_example.php
array (
  'name' => 'London',
  'country' => 'GB',
  'population' => 8174100,
)
```

We can see from our test console that the stored value is rather memcache them specific and likely to be incompatible with standard usage.

```
hazelcast[default] > m.entries
London-GB : MemcacheEntry{bytes=VALUE London-GB 1 81
a:3:{s:4:"name";s:6:"London";s:7:"country";s:2:"GB";s:10:"population"
;i:8174100;}
, flag=1}
Total 1
```

But we are benefiting from Hazelcast's inbuilt data distribution and resilience, and we can manage the cluster as we normally would, scaling as required. The only disadvantage of that flexibility compared to standard memcaching; is that we must be careful not to remove all the nodes to which the client is expecting to be there as part of its static configuration.

Going RESTful

An alternative to memcache would be the even more generic **RESTful** API. Without wanting to go into too much detail, **REST** is a popular convention of providing HTTP access to data via resources; these are set up to provide path-like access to collections, objects, and properties. Hazelcast additionally provides a simple HTTP service built-in to each of the nodes to enable access to our standard map and queue collections via HTTP.

The structure of the API is pretty simple:

```
http://127.0.0.1:5701/hazelcast/rest/maps/mapName/key
```

```
http://127.0.0.1:5701/hazelcast/rest/queues/queueName
```

Where `mapName` or `queueName` is as configured within our application, we can then use the standard REST convention of using the HTTP method to describe the type of operation we wish to perform.

In the case of maps, we send in all cases the appropriate **key** as required; but using a `POST` method to create or update an entry, specifying an appropriate **MIME** type as needed.

```
$ curl -v -X POST -H "Content-Type: text/plain" -d "bar" \
http://127.0.0.1:5701/hazelcast/rest/maps/test/foo

< HTTP/1.1 204 No Content
< Content-Length: 0
```

We use a `GET` method to retrieve an entry, returning a `200 OK` response for keys that hold a value and `204 No Content` for keys that do not. The appropriate MIME type that was specified when setting the data will be returned.

```
$ curl -X GET \
http://127.0.0.1:5701/hazelcast/rest/maps/test/foo

< HTTP/1.1 200 OK
< Content-Type: text/plain
< Content-Length: 3

bar
```

And a `DELETE` method to remove an entry, unless there is an error, this method will always return a `No Content` response irrespective of whether the data existed or not.

```
$ curl -v -X DELETE \
http://127.0.0.1:5701/hazelcast/rest/maps/test/foo
```

```
< HTTP/1.1 204 No Content
< Content-Length: 0
```

With queues it is slightly simpler as we only have two operations we can perform on the queue; pushing and popping. Like maps we use `POST` to create an item on the queue.

```
$ curl -v -X POST -H "Content-Type: text/plain" -d "foo" \
http://127.0.0.1:5701/hazelcast/rest/queues/myEvents
```

```
< HTTP/1.1 204 No Content
< Content-Length: 0
```

For the case of retrieving we use `DELETE` as this gets, removes, and returns all in one; we should also pass an extra path parameter when polling for queue events so as to indicate the poll timeout.

```
$ curl -v -X DELETE \
http://127.0.0.1:5701/hazelcast/rest/queues/myEvents/10
```

```
< HTTP/1.1 200 OK
< Content-Type: text/plain
< Content-Length: 3
```

```
foo
```

In the case of the timeout being reached, we are returned a `No Content` success indicating there was no item present on the queue to return.

```
$ curl -v -X DELETE \
http://127.0.0.1:5701/hazelcast/rest/queues/myEvents/10
```

```
< HTTP/1.1 204 No Content
< Content-Length: 0
```

We do need to make sure that we appropriately handle the various HTTP error conditions as the REST API is not transactional, and we will need to either retry or trigger the correct error handling logic within our application.

Like the memcache companion API, RESTbased access is best used solely on collections accessed using this method and in conjunction with storing only string based or simple primitive values. Attempting to access a more complex object (perhaps one created via the standard Java client) while that might functionally work, you will not get the answer that you expect (most likely a binary serialized blob). However, map DELETE operations will still largely work uninhibited, this is because they don't return the actual value.

Cluster status via REST

One last bit of useful access via REST is to obtain the cluster state and logging information. There are two resources that return such information from outside the cluster. This could be very helpful in setting up external monitoring of the cluster from tools such as **Nagios**.

```
$ curl -v http://127.0.0.1:5701/hazelcast/rest/cluster

< HTTP/1.1 200 OK
< Content-Length: 119

Cluster [2] {
  Member [192.168.1.77]:5701 this
  Member [192.168.1.77]:5702
}

ConnectionCount: 2
AllConnectionCount: 8


$ curl -v http://127.0.0.1:5701/hazelcast/rest/dump

< HTTP/1.1 200 OK
< Content-Type: text/plain
< Content-Length: 128723
```

REST resilience

As we can use the REST API present on any of the nodes to access the cluster's stored data, this makes it a perfect candidate for placing behind an HTTP load balancer and/or HTTPS wrapping layer to provide additional resilience or security. As each operation we perform on a particular node is translated to a cluster-wide operation, even if we use load-balancing mechanisms such as round robin, the consistency of the replication will ensure that the correct values are served.

Summary

We have seen that Hazelcast isn't a closed technology, while it draws from its own Java-centric background, and is best placed to support applications based on that stack; it does allow more generic access to the cluster's data. Inspired by other standards and conventions already present in the wider community, Hazelcast has avoided completely reinventing the wheel and has found an ideal mix to complement its own offering but also allow existing applications to migrate across easily.

In the next chapter we shall look at taking our application into the cloud and the differences when deploying on a public cloud infrastructure.

9
Going Global

As we have seen, Hazelcast provides us with a dynamic data and processing backbone to build an application around us. However, recently we have seen the rise of cloud computing. More-and-more applications are designed to work in conjunction with it and have started embracing this new approach to infrastructure. In this chapter, we shall look at:

- Newfound problems with cluster discovery in the cloud world
- Manual specific or nomination node approach
- Cloud provider specific solutions
- Spreading out around the world

Getting setup in the cloud

All of our examples so far have relied on the standard default cluster discovery process. This uses an IP multicast approach, allowing each new node to interrogate the local network to discover any preexisting clusters, and request to join it should it match an expected configuration. One notable feature of public cloud infrastructures is that they tend to share a common network between multiple customers on their virtualized hardware. To avoid any security concerns, distributed networking capabilities such as multicast tend to be blocked; as such we need another mechanism of cluster discovery.

There are two other ways of configuring a cluster:

- Manual seeded unicast configuration
- Discovery supported by Amazon AWS management APIs

Under manual control

In a very similar manner to the way we previously used a thin client to connect to the cluster rather than automatically discovering it, we can nominate a number of nodes that can be used to discover the presence of the wider cluster. This is akin to registering a node's presence with a set of arbiters; then using them to both find existing peers and distributing the appearance of that new node to others in the cluster. There is a higher expectation of availability of the nodes used in this role. Should all of them fail, no new node will be able to join the cluster without adjusting their configuration to address this situation.

So the process works a bit like this. When the **10.0.0.101** node attempts to connect to the cluster that is configured with the knowledge, it should expect peers to exist at **10.0.0.1** and **10.0.0.2**. Once it has successfully connected to either of these, it can learn about the rest of the topology of the cluster and establish the required connections as appropriate.

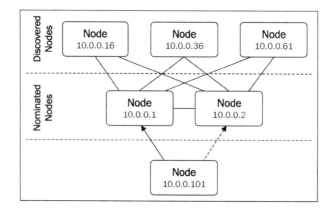

As this process only requires regular IP unicast to work, it only requires the same level of networking capabilities as the needs of supporting the cluster generally; so this process will always be able to work wherever the cluster can. The primary disadvantage is the static nature of the configuration, but infrastructure automation technologies (such as Puppet or Chef) might help mitigate this limitation.

To configure this, we can modify our `hazelcast.xml` file to specify the appropriate configuration. We can use the hostname or IP addresses/ranges to define the potential seed nodes to connect to. The default port of **5701** is assumed unless it is overridden.

```
<hazelcast>
  <network>
    <join>
      <tcp-ip enabled="true">
        <hostname>targethost</hostname>
```

```
        <hostname>otherhost:5702</hostname>
        <interface>10.0.0.1</interface>
        <interface>10.0.0.1-2</interface>
      </tcp-ip>
    </join>
  </network>
</hazelcast>
```

Discovery – the Amazonian way

Like we mentioned in the previous section, the network fabric supporting the public cloud infrastructure tends to avoid allowing low-level network features that create the possibility of security concerns; this includes broadcast and multicast. However, in the case of Amazon's AWS elastic cloud offering, there are quite a few custom API services that can be used to programmatically control and integrate what has been deployed. To enable non-static but non-multicast discovery, a wrapper to specifically harness EC2's management APIs has been created, and is provided as part of the `hazelcast-cloud-2.6.jar` file.

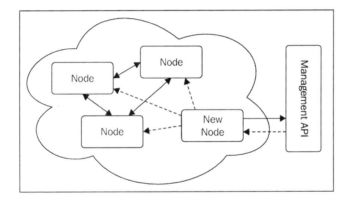

Using this, we can configure this capability once this package has been added to the classpath, using the following configuration:

```
<hazelcast>
  <network>
    <join>
      <aws enabled="true">
        <access-key>ourApiAccessKey</access-key>
        <secret-key>ourApiSecretKey</secret-key>
        <region>eu-west-1</region>
        <!-- optionally to filter results -->
        <security-group-name>hazelcast-sg</security-group-name>
```

```
            <tag-key>server-type</tag-key>
            <tag-value>hazelcast-node</tag-value>

        </aws>
      </join>
    </network>
</hazelcast>
```

The configuration of this discovery mechanism is very much specific to how we use and set up our application within the cloud infrastructure. The access key and secret key are provided via the **Security Credentials** section of your account in the management console, provisioning a new pair if required.

When creating an access key, we will be provided with a text file download containing the API key identifier, which is a secret key. It is these values we need to insert into our configuration to provide authentication to the supporting discovery API.

```
AWSAccessKeyId=AKIAJCC2OT7LRVJTG3QQ

AWSSecretKey=ibfh3UMkSOhJNmoytK/46Q+2juhbJ61KczE+Z43P
```

The region property should correspond to where your application is deployed (and defaults to **us-east-1** if not specified). Unlike our previous manual seeded option, we don't have the ability to run on custom ports so any application that must be running on the default port will be discovered. It would be prudent to disable the port auto-incrementing functionality within our configuration so this doesn't become an issue.

```
<hazelcast>
  <network>
    <port auto-increment="false">5701</port>
  </network>
</hazelcast>
```

Filtering the possibilities

Once we configure the appropriate security credentials and regions, we shall have a functioning discovery process in place. However, should we have a large number of server instances running within our account that are not intending to run Hazelcast, we might find that the node startup process can be rather slow as we try unsuccessfully to connect to the irrelevant servers not running Hazelcast. To avoid this, we have two options at our disposal.

Firstly, AWS provides a way of defining a standard set of network security policies for a collection of server-like instances; these are known as **security groups**. It is considered the best practice to place servers of common types or functions within the same group. Should we do this for our cluster nodes, we have just to add the security-group-name to our configuration, and only servers within this group shall be considered as potential cluster nodes. Secondly, we have the capability of tagging EC2 instances with a number of custom key values. Should we have our own defined tag to mark a server instance as running a Hazelcast node, we can use the tag key and the tag value to inform the node discovery process of this custom configuration.

Spreading out around the globe

To enable true resilience for our application, the standard approach to handling disaster recovery is to set up a duplicate instance in another data center. Typically, these should be apart far enough to ensure that if any local event significant in stature might impact our standard operations, then at least one of our data centers should not be affected. Irrespective of our requirements of recovery time and recovery point, we will need a process for migrating data between our sites, so that should there be a need to fall over to an alternative site, we will have the required data there ready for us.

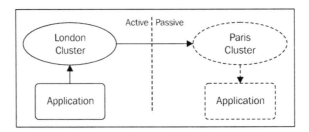

We can configure Hazelcast to push entries from our local cluster to a remote cluster by defining a **WAN (Wide Area Network)** replication policy. So, we add a policy to push changes to Paris to our London configuration.

```
<hazelcast>
  <wan-replication name="our-global-cluster">
    <target-cluster group-name="paris" group-password="paris-pass">

      <replication-impl>
        com.hazelcast.impl.wan.WanNoDelayReplication
      </replication-impl>

      <end-points>
        <address>12.34.56.78:5701</address>
      </end-points>

    </target-cluster>
  </wan-replication>
</hazelcast>
```

This would produce an active-passive setup, as entries created on the London cluster would be replicated across to paris. But as paris is not configured to push any changes made on its cluster back to London, it can be considered a pre-warmed ready standby cluster, which while not normally active can take over should there exist an issue with the primary site.

However, we could go one stage further and enable full active-active replication. To do this, we would have to update the configuration on our **Paris Cluster** to also replicate back to London. In this way, both sites can operate at the same time and will update each other with the changes made on each of them. But doing so introduces an issue — as each cluster operates independently, we have enabled the possibility of a race condition on setting of data. So, when the global replication kicks in and the data is exported between them, we could have two versions of the same data. This is a similar situation to the Split-brain networking issue we previously encountered. To address this problem, we use exactly the same solution as before; by configuring a consistent merge policy, we can define how to select which version of the data is the one to keep.

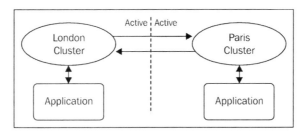

As we may wish to tactfully select which collections are actually replicated between the sites, we need to add an additional configuration to each data collection configuration (or the default) to enable the replication. We also configure the appropriate merge policy within each configuration, enabling the ability to vary it for differing collections.

```
<hazelcast>
  <map name="default">

    <wan-replication-ref name="our-global-cluster">
      <merge-policy>hz.LATEST_UPDATE</merge-policy>
    </wan-replication-ref>
  </map>

</hazelcast>
```

We can use any of the merge policies we have previously seen, or as before define our own if needed.

Summary

One of the greatest features of Hazelcast is its distributed scalability. We have now seen that this isn't just limited to our own servers or data center. We can spread out to run our application cluster on public cloud infrastructures, and even on multiple sites around the world, and through the use of an active-active deployment, our application can truly go global.

In the next and final chapter, we shall look at how Hazelcast can collaborate with the existing technology stacks, both at the application and data layers.

10
Playing Well with Others

Technology stacks have evolved into precise and broad choices, with numerous libraries and their dependencies all bundled together to support our applications. To help integrate into this wild ecosystem of technologies, Hazelcast provides us with some support to use and extend a few popularly used libraries.

In this chapter we shall cover:

- Using dependency injection to help set up our cluster
- Working with a popular data layer for caching to help bridge the gap between traditional databases and the new world of Hazelcast
- Using external database persistence for Hazelcast collections to bridge the gap back in the opposite direction
- Providing an alternative distributed session store for web applications
- Introducing the cluster management center

Don't pass what you need, depend on it

Most of the examples we have developed so far have created `HazelcastInstance` that we use to programmatically access various collections and features of the cluster. However as we begin to move away from simple conceptual examples, we will need to start passing references to various collections around our application in order to access data. This exposes the age-old problem of how to avoid passing around supporting dependencies around the application layers, but still having access to them, when and where they are required. Luckily this problem has already been solved for us in the form of *dependency injection*. Rather than reinventing the wheel, we should be able to use the existing technology to help solve this problem.

One of the most popular **DI** frameworks is **Spring**, and Hazelcast features complimentary support for this framework allowing us to configure our cluster in a way in keeping with it. To enable this support we need to add the `hazelcast-spring-2.6.jar` package to our spring-enabled classpath and in doing so we can add a Hazelcast specific namespace to our Spring configuration.

```
<beans xmlns="http://www.springframework.org/schema/beans"
  xmlns:xsi="http://www.w3.org/2001/XMLSchema-instance"
  xmlns:hz="http://www.hazelcast.com/schema/spring"
  xsi:schemaLocation="http://www.springframework.org/schema/beans
    http://www.springframework.org/schema/beans/spring-beans-3.2.xsd
    http://www.hazelcast.com/schema/spring
    http://www.hazelcast.com/schema/spring/hazelcast-spring-2.5.xsd">
```

This will provide us with an `hz` namespace to allow us to now configure our cluster, clients, and collections as required using an XML file used as part of the standard Spring application's context configuration.

```
<beans>
  <hz:hazelcast id="hzInstance">
    <hz:config>
      <hz:group name="london" password="london-pass"/>

      <hz:wan-replication name="our-global-cluster">
        <hz:target-cluster
          group-name="paris"
          group-password="paris-pass">
          <hz:replication-impl>
            com.hazelcast.impl.wan.WanNoDelayReplication
          </hz:replication-impl>
          <hz:end-points>
            <hz:address>12.34.56.78</hz:address>
          </hz:end-points>
        </hz:target-cluster>
      </hz:wan-replication>

      <hz:network port="5701" port-auto-increment="false">
        <hz:join>
          <hz:multicast
            enabled="true"
            multicast-group="224.2.2.3"
            multicast-port="54327"/>
        </hz:join>
      </hz:network>
```

```
        <hz:map
          name="default"
          backup-count="2"
          read-backup-data="true"
          merge-policy="hz.LATEST_UPDATE">
          <hz:wan-replication-ref
            name="our-global-cluster"
            merge-policy="hz.LATEST_UPDATE"/>
        </hz:map>

      </hz:config>
    </hz:hazelcast>
</beans>
```

As we can see, the structure of the Spring namespace is very much inspired by the standard hazelcast.xml configuration; admittedly some of the property elements have been moved to be attributes, but we should be able to use our IDE in conjunction with the XSD file to navigate through the structure.

Once defined, we can obtain a reference to the configured HazelcastInstance using Spring's standard application context.

```
HazelcastInstance hz =
    (HazelcastInstance)applicationContext.getBean("hzInstance");
IMap<String, String> capitals = hz.getMap("capitals");
```

For cases where rather than creating a full node instance we want to use the native thin client, we can also configure this in a similar way:

```
<hz:client id="hzInstance"
  group-name="london"
  group-password="london-pass">

  <hz:member>127.0.0.1:5701</hz:member>
</hz:client>
```

Simplifying collection access

However, to help simplify our application's code we can also configure Spring to provide access to collection beans directly. The inbuilt namespace allows us to do this with a number of the possible distributed collections.

We can configure the standard collections as follows:

```
<hz:map id="mapBean" instance-ref="hzInstance" name="mapName" />
<hz:set id="setBean" instance-ref="hzInstance" name="setName" />
<hz:list id="listBean" instance-ref="hzInstance"
```

```
    name="listName" />
<hz:queue id="queueBean" instance-ref="hzInstance"
  name="queueName" />
<hz:multiMap id="multiMapBean" instance-ref="hzInstance"
  name="multiMapName" />
<hz:topic id="topicBean" instance-ref="hzInstance"
  name="topicName" />
<hz:atomicNumber id="lockBean" instance-ref="hzInstance"

  name="lockName"/>
```

We can also configure some of the more advanced capabilities we have looked at.

```
<hz:executorService id="executorServiceBean"
  instance-ref="hzInstance" name="executorServiceName" />
<hz:idGenerator id="idGeneratorBean" instance-ref="hzInstance"

  name="idGeneratorName" />
```

Just like before, we can use the application context to inject references to the configured collections themselves, without having to inject the Hazelcast instance.

```
<hz:map id="capitalsMap" instance-ref="hzInstance"
  name="capitals" />

IMap<String, String> capitals =
  (IMap)applicationContext.getBean("capitalsMap");
```

We can even use the annotation-driven-based bean injecting, however be aware that due to a Spring bug this causes the client application to copy the entire map from the cluster to a local instance, which given the possible data sizes involved is very inefficient. To avoid this, we simply have to inject a non-generic version of the collection.

```
public class CapitalCityService {

  @Autowired
  private IMap capitals;

}
```

Transparently caching others' data

Another very popularly used framework is **Hibernate**, used as an **ORM (Object Relationship Mapper)** layer, traditionally used to translate objects to and from a relational database table. While this goes against the distributed data philosophy we have been exploring with Hazelcast, we may have a legacy application that is currently using it. By adding a caching layer we can improve the scalability and performance of this application, however by enabling this cache layer we will be introducing a data consistency issue; to avoid this we would need an intelligent distributed cache, exactly like Hazelcast.

To enable the use of the cache layer, we must again include the appropriate `hazelcast-hibernate-2.6.jar` extension to the classpath. Additionally we need to turn on Hibernate's second level caching functionality and define the Hazelcast region-caching wrapper within its `hibernate.cfg.xml` configuration.

```
<hibernate-configuration>
  <session-factory>

    <property name="hibernate.cache.use_second_level_cache">
      true
    </property>

    <property name="hibernate.cache.region.factory_class">
      com.hazelcast.hibernate.HazelcastCacheRegionFactory
    </property>
  </session-factory>
</hibernate-configuration>
```

Should we be using an older classic version of the Hibernate framework that does not feature cache regions (versions older than 3.3), we can use the previous terminology and supported configuration of the cache provider.

```
<hibernate-configuration>
  <session-factory>

    <property name="hibernate.cache.provider_class">
      com.hazelcast.hibernate.provider.HazelcastCacheProvider
    </property>
  </session-factory>
</hibernate-configuration>
```

While this enables the second level cache at a high level, we also need to configure individual entities to be cached, as they aren't by default. We can do this via an HBM mapping XML.

```
<hibernate-mapping>
  <class name="com.packtpub.hazelcast.chapter10.hibernate.City"
table="city">
    <cache region="city" usage="read-write"/>

    <id name="name" column="name" type="string">
    <property name="country" column="country" type="string"/>
    <property name="population" column="population" type="int"/>
  </class>
</hibernate-mapping>
```

Or, if we are using JPA and annotation based entity mappings, we can use the @ Cache annotation on our entity class itself.

```
@Entity(name = "city")
@Cache(region = "city", usage =
  CacheConcurrencyStrategy.READ_WRITE)
public class City implements Serializable {
```

The region name is used by the Hazelcast cache implementation and it is this value that is used to define the distributed map name where cache entries will be held. We can configure these cache maps in the same way as we would do for any other map, should we wish to have specific behavior on these collections.

Hibernate provides us with the ability to use one of the four caching strategies for entities, however, not all are supported by Hazelcast. The three possible options are:

- Read-only
    - The best performing strategy for data that is read frequently but never changes

- Read-write
    - When our cached data needs to be updated and might be quite frequently

- Nonstrict-read-write
    - A performance compromise where data is read most frequently but might be rarely updated and certainly not concurrently

Bring your own cluster

By default we will spin up a new Hazelcast node as part of the Hibernate cache provider; however, we may not wish to do so. We can connect to a pre-existing cluster in a number of different ways.

Firstly we can switch the provider created instance into a lite-member, so that rather than participating in the storage of clusters we can join it for access.

```
<hibernate-configuration>
  <session-factory>

    <property name="hibernate.cache.hazelcast.use_lite_member">
      true
    </property>
  </session-factory>
</hibernate-configuration>
```

The next option we have at our disposal is we can use the native thin client to connect to an external cluster rather than a full or lite instance that joins as a member node.

```
<hibernate-configuration>
  <session-factory>

  <property name="hibernate.cache.hazelcast.native_client_address">
    127.0.0.1
  </property>
  <property name="hibernate.cache.hazelcast.native_client_group">
    dev
  </property>
  <property
    name="hibernate.cache.hazelcast.native_client_password">
   dev-pass
  </property>
  </session-factory>
</hibernate-configuration>
```

Lastly, should we have already created a Hazelcast instance within our application, rather than create a second one for caching we can provide the existing one with a name and pass that instance name over to the Hibernate cache provider; this enables the existing instance to be looked up through the use of the helper function `Hazelcast.getHazelcastInstanceByName(String)`.

```
<hibernate-configuration>
  <session-factory>
```

```
      <property name="hibernate.cache.hazelcast.instance_name">
        my-existing-instance
      </property>
    </session-factory>
</hibernate-configuration>
```

Cacheable methods with the Spring cache

While the caching layer provided as part of Hibernate unlocks easy and convenient caching for high frequency or high cost data; but what about at a higher level and more generally, method calls can be expensive too.

Newer versions of the Spring framework (since version 3.1) features the ability to transparently cache method calls and their returned results, through the use of the `com.hazelcast.spring.cache.HazelcastCacheManager` class, and its registration as a Spring cache manager.

```
<cache:annotation-driven cache-manager="cacheManager" />

<bean id="cacheManager"
  class="com.hazelcast.spring.cache.HazelcastCacheManager">

  <constructor-arg ref="hzInstance"/>
</bean>
```

With this in place, we can then mark appropriate methods as `@Cacheable` and where required use `@CacheEvict` to trigger cache invalidations.

Collection persistence

Just as using Hazelcast to provide a distributed caching layer in front of our traditional database, we can also invert this relationship. By having Hazelcast as the primary data store we can configure `MapStore` to provide long term persistence of stored objects, working around the potential risk of data resilience due to Hazelcast's in-memory nature.

This resilience, however, does come at a cost to performance and scalability. This means that we have to update an external system upon each change to the cluster data. However, we can configure the method of this process between synchronous (where data is written out to the store prior to returning confirmation to the client), or asynchronous (where this process happens in the background shortly after) through the use of the `write-delay-seconds` configuration. A zero value indicates synchronous persistence and a positive value determines the delay before the asynchronous process kicks in.

So an example map configuration would look something like this:

```
<map name="default">

  <map-store enabled="true">
    <class-name>
      com.hazelcast.examples.DummyStore
    </class-name>

    <write-delay-seconds>0</write-delay-seconds>
  </map-store>
</map>
```

We will need to provide our own implementation of MapStore (rather than the example DummyStore as shown in the preceding code) and to avoid a potential deadlock must not persist back into Hazelcast, which would rather defeat the point anyway.

Web session storage

Another complementary piece of functionality is the ability to provide session persistence to a web application. These are normally provided by the application container, but these typically have replication or scalability issues with large deployments. This problem tends to be addressed through the use of "sticky sessions" where a load balancer sitting in front of the application routes related traffic through to the same container; but what would happen in a failure situation? If the container did not feature any form of replication, the session would be lost and a negative customer experience would be encountered.

Hazelcast can help address this issue by providing an external and distributed session store for our application. By including hazelcast-wm-2.6.jar in our web application and configuring the web.xml file, we can provide session persistence using a web application filter. In the case that your application uses multiple filters, make sure that this is the first filter defined within the configuration.

```
<listener>
  <listener-class>com.hazelcast.web.SessionListener</listener-class>
</listener>

<filter>
  <filter-name>hazelcast-filter</filter-name>
  <filter-class>com.hazelcast.web.WebFilter</filter-class>

  <init-param>
```

```
      <param-name>map-name</param-name>
      <param-value>session-store</param-value>
    </init-param>

    <init-param>
      <param-name>session-ttl-seconds</param-name>
      <param-value>86400</param-value>
    </init-param>

    <init-param>
      <param-name>cookie-name</param-name>
      <param-value>sessionId</param-value>
    </init-param>

    <init-param>
      <param-name>cookie-domain</param-name>
      <param-value>.packtpub.com</param-value>
    </init-param>

    <init-param>
      <param-name>config-location</param-name>
      <param-value>/WEB-INF/hazelcast.xml</param-value>
    </init-param>
  </filter>

  <filter-mapping>
    <filter-name>hazelcast-filter</filter-name>
    <url-pattern>/*</url-pattern>
    <dispatcher>FORWARD</dispatcher>
    <dispatcher>INCLUDE</dispatcher>
    <dispatcher>REQUEST</dispatcher>
  </filter-mapping>
```

Should we already have Hazelcast as part of our application, we can use the instance naming capability to access that existing one; replacing the `config-location` initial parameter with one that names the appropriate instance.

```
  <init-param>
    <param-name>instance-name</param-name>
    <param-value>my-existing-instance</param-value>
  </init-param>
```

Management center

Throughout this book we have seen how to set up and use Hazelcast to support our application, but once we start using it we will need to maintain and support our cluster. While we are able to gain great insight into the goings on programmatically, that would take some effort to capture and control all aspects of the cluster. A part of our downloaded archive is Hazelcast's own management center (`mancenter-2.6.war`) which provides access to cluster and collection information as well as management capabilities. While this is a commercial product, it is currently free to be used with up to a two-node cluster.

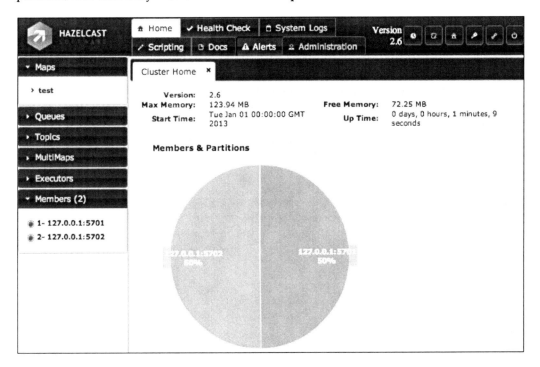

Summary

Here we can see that Hazelcast has yet again attempted to integrate well into a software library eco-system, knowing that the same wheel has already been invented in order to solve various problems or provide particular functionality. Being able to work well with other popular frameworks allows us to bring in this new world of thinking into our existing stack a much smoother process.

As we have seen throughout, the technology provides us with a flexible, extensible, and dynamic data source enabling us to build data stores and structures that are truly distributed without any single point of failure. We can use various generic collections to hold our data in appropriate ways, be it for key value storage, FIFO queuing, or providing a mechanism for a cluster wide communication topic. It also provides us with additional complimentary capabilities that would normally be crow-barred into other centralized services (for example, using database row locking for cluster locks or de-duplicating task processing to multiple executor services). However what makes this technology truly great is its incredibly low barrier to entry (something I hope we have discovered throughout this journey); now we just need to expand out into our applications in the real world and we'll further appreciate the amazing power we are bringing to it.

Configuration Summary

Throughout this book we have progressively listed a number of configurations used to customize and modify the behavior of the Hazelcast cluster; here we bring them together as a quick reference.

XML configuration

The following is a complete example of the `hazelcast.xml` configuration file with an overview of each section within it:

```
<hazelcast>
```

Cluster name

```
<group>
  <name>dev</name>
  <password>dev-pass</password>
</group>
```

Management Center

```
<management-center enabled="true" update-interval="5">
  http://manager-center-host:8080/mancenter
</management-center>
```

General Properties

```
<properties>
  <property name="hazelcast.map.partition.count">271</property>
</properties>
```

WAN replication configuration

```
<wan-replication name="our-global-cluster">
  <target-cluster group-name="paris" group-password="paris-pass">

    <replication-impl>
      com.hazelcast.impl.wan.WanNoDelayReplication
    </replication-impl>
    <end-points>
      <address>12.34.56.78:5701</address>
    </end-points>

  </target-cluster>
</wan-replication>
```

Local network/interface binding

```
<network>
  <port auto-increment="false">5701</port>

  <interfaces enabled="true">
    <interface>192.168.0.*</interface>
  </interfaces>
```

Cluster discovery

Multicast, Unicast, or EC2-based

```
<join>
  <multicast enabled="true">
    <multicast-group>224.2.2.3</multicast-group>
    <multicast-port>54327</multicast-port>
  </multicast>
  <tcp-ip enabled="true">
    <interface>127.0.0.1</interface>
```

```
      </tcp-ip>
      <aws enabled="true">
        <access-key>ourApiAccessKey</access-key>
        <secret-key>ourApiSecretKey</secret-key>
        <region>eu-west-1</region>
      </aws>
    </join>
  </network>
```

Per map or default map configuration

```
    <map name="capitals">
```

cluster_wide_map_size
partitions_wide_map_size
max_size_per_jvm
used_heap_size
used_heap_percentage
```
      <max-size policy="cluster_wide_map_size">10</max-size>
```

LRU: Least Recently Used

LFU: Least Frequently Used

NONE

```
      <eviction-policy>LFU</eviction-policy>
      <eviction-percentage>20</eviction-percentage>
```

Backup = Synchronous copies
Async = Asynchronous copies
Total copies = 1 Main + Backup + Async
```
      <backup-count>1</backup-count>
      <async-backup-count>1</async-backup-count>
```

Age expiry and idle expiry times

```
      <time-to-live-seconds>86400</time-to-live-seconds>
      <max-idle-seconds>3600</max-idle-seconds>
```

hz.NO_MERGE
hz.ADD_NEW_ENTRY

hz.HIGHER_HITS

hz.LATEST_UPDATE

```
<merge-policy>hz.LATEST_UPDATE</merge-policy>
```

Selected WAN replication configuration

```
<wan-replication-ref name="our-global-cluster">
  <merge-policy> hz.LATEST_UPDATE </merge-policy>
</wan-replication-ref>
```

Indexes on values

```
<indexes>
  <index ordered="false">name</index>
  <index ordered="true">population</index>
</indexes>
```

Listeners notified on map events

```
<entry-listeners>
  <entry-listener include-value="true" local="false">
    com.packtpub.hazelcast.listeners.MapEntryListener
  </entry-listener>
</entry-listeners>

</map>
```

Listener notified on topic broadcast

```
<topic name="default">
  <message-listeners>
    <message-listener>
      com.hazelcast.examples.MessageListener
    </message-listener>
  </message-listeners>
</topic>
```

Cluster-wide listener registration

```
<listeners>
  <listener>
    com.packtpub.hazelcast.listeners.TopicListener
  </listener>
</listeners>

</hazelcast>
```

Programmatic configuration

As we saw within the book, it is also possible to configure Hazelcast programmatically, this can provide for a higher application control of the cluster.

```
Config conf = new Config();
```

Set general properties

```
conf.setProperty("hazelcast.map.partition.count", "271");
```

Set instance name

```
conf.setInstanceName("my-instance");
```

Set as lite member

```
conf.setLiteMember(true);
```

Get reference to map configuration

```
MapConfig citiesConf = conf.getMapConfig("cities");
```

Modify default behavior

```
citiesConf.setBackupCount(2);
citiesConf.setAsyncBackupCount(1);
```

Add map index

```
citiesConf.addMapIndexConfig(
  new MapIndexConfig("country", false));
```

Index

de facto leader 10
deployment, Hazelcast 77
distributed cache 11
distributed executor service
  about 67
  accessing 68, 69
distributed locking
  about 34-36
  tactical locking 36
distributed map collection 33, 34

E

entryEvicted method 56
EntryListener 55, 56
equals() method 27
eviction-percentage 31
eviction-policy 30
ExecutorService 67
expanded architecture 9

F

first-in first-out (FIFO) 23

G

get() function 70

H

hashCode() method 27
Hazelcast
  about 10
  atomic control 33
  basic application, creating 16-20
  broadcast messaging system 41
  capabilities 12
  cluster, scaling up 50
  collection listeners, creating 55
  collection listeners, using 55
  collection persistence 108
  data, backing up 48, 49
  data, spilting into partitions 47
  data, within heap of nodes 77
  deployment 77
  distributed locking 34
  distributed map collection 33

downloading 15, 16
features 10, 11
integrating, with Hibernate 105-107
integrating, with Spring 101-103
limitation 85
limits, setting 29, 30
management center 111
memcache 85
MultiMap collection 24
network partitioning 52-54
nodes, grouping 50-52
nodes, seperating 50-52
programmatic configuration 59, 117
RESTful 88
setting up, in cloud world 93
storage collections, exploring 22-24
transactional capabilities 37
using, within enterprise J2EE container 40
web session storage 109
XML configuration 113
HazelcastInstanceAware interface 69
Hibernate
  caching strategies 106
hybrid cluster 83

I

IdGenerator 40
include-value flag 58
indexing 26
InstanceListener 55, 59
ItemListener 55, 58

K

keyless collections 58

L

LifecycleListener 55, 61
lite cluster members 80, 81

M

management center 111
MapEntryListener 56
masterless distributed cluster 11
max-idle-seconds 31

Thank you for buying
Getting Started with Hazelcast

About Packt Publishing

Packt, pronounced 'packed', published its first book "*Mastering phpMyAdmin for Effective MySQL Management*" in April 2004 and subsequently continued to specialize in publishing highly focused books on specific technologies and solutions.

Our books and publications share the experiences of your fellow IT professionals in adapting and customizing today's systems, applications, and frameworks. Our solution based books give you the knowledge and power to customize the software and technologies you're using to get the job done. Packt books are more specific and less general than the IT books you have seen in the past. Our unique business model allows us to bring you more focused information, giving you more of what you need to know, and less of what you don't.

Packt is a modern, yet unique publishing company, which focuses on producing quality, cutting-edge books for communities of developers, administrators, and newbies alike. For more information, please visit our website: www.packtpub.com.

About Packt Open Source

In 2010, Packt launched two new brands, Packt Open Source and Packt Enterprise, in order to continue its focus on specialization. This book is part of the Packt Open Source brand, home to books published on software built around Open Source licences, and offering information to anybody from advanced developers to budding web designers. The Open Source brand also runs Packt's Open Source Royalty Scheme, by which Packt gives a royalty to each Open Source project about whose software a book is sold.

Writing for Packt

We welcome all inquiries from people who are interested in authoring. Book proposals should be sent to author@packtpub.com. If your book idea is still at an early stage and you would like to discuss it first before writing a formal book proposal, contact us; one of our commissioning editors will get in touch with you.

We're not just looking for published authors; if you have strong technical skills but no writing experience, our experienced editors can help you develop a writing career, or simply get some additional reward for your expertise.

Infinispan Data Grid Platform

ISBN: 978-1-84951-8-222   Paperback: 150 pages

Making use of data grids for performance and scalability in Enterprise Java, using Infinispan from JBoss

1. Configure and develop applications using the Infinispan Data grid platform

2. Follow a simple ticket booking example to easily learn the features of Infinispan in practice

3. Draw on the experience of Manik Surtani, the leader, architect and founder of this popular open source project

JBoss AS 7 Configuration, Deployment and Administration

ISBN: 978-1-84951-6-785   Paperback: 380 pages

Build a fully-functional, efficient application server using JBoss AS

1. Covers all JBoss AS 7 administration topics in a concise, practical, and understandable manner, along with detailed explanations and lots of screenshots

2. Uncover the advanced features of JBoss AS, including High Availability and clustering, integration with other frameworks, and creating complex AS domain configurations

3. Discover the new features of JBoss AS 7, which has made quite a departure from previous versions

Please check **www.PacktPub.com** for information on our titles

open source
community experience distilled

JBoss ESB Beginner's Guide

ISBN: 978-1-84951-6-587   Paperback: 320 pages

A comprehensive, practical guide to developing service-based applications using the Open Source JBoss Enterprise Service Bus

1. Develop your own service-based applications, from simple deployments through to complex legacy integrations

2. Learn how services can communicate with each other and the benefits to be gained from loose coupling

3. Contains clear, practical instructions for service development, highlighted through the use of numerous working examples

Drools Developer's Cookbook

ISBN: 978-1-84951-1-964   Paperback: 310 pages

Over 40 recipes for creating a robust business rules implementation by using JBoss Drools rules

1. Master the newest Drools Expert, Fusion, Guvnor, Planner and jBPM5 features

2. Integrate Drools by using popular Java Frameworks

3. Part of Packt's Cookbook series: each recipe is independent and contains practical, step-by-step instructions to help you achieve your goal.

Please check **www.PacktPub.com** for information on our titles

Lightning Source UK Ltd.
Milton Keynes UK
UKOW02f0712171013

219159UK00002B/81/P